our place

our place

Kanika Ambrose

our place
first published 2023 by Scirocco Drama
An imprint of J. Gordon Shillingford Publishing Inc.

Scirocco Drama Editor: Glenda MacFarlane
Cover design by Doowah Design
Author Photo by Dahlia Katz
Cover photo of Virgilia Griffith and all production photos by Gesilayefa Azorbo

Printed and bound in Canada on 100% post-consumer recycled paper.

Production Information:
Ian Arnold, Catalyst Talent Creative Management
ian@catalysttcm.com
416-568-8673

Future productions should contact Alicia for her use of her resource kit on dialects: Alicia.dionne.richardson@gmail.com

Future productions should contact DJ L'Oqenz, the original Sound Designer/Composer, for use of her original compositions c/o Dave Guenette daveg@piratesblend.com

Library and Archives Canada Cataloguing in Publication

Title: Our place / Kanika Ambrose.
Names: Ambrose, Kanika, author.
Identifiers: Canadiana (print) 20230519121 | Canadiana (ebook) 20230519156 | ISBN 9781990738265 (softcover) | ISBN 9781990738371 (EPUB)
Subjects: LCGFT: Drama.
Classification: LCC PS8601.M3774 O97 2023 | DDC C812/.6—dc23

We acknowledge the financial support of the Canada Council for the Arts, the Government of Canada, the Manitoba Arts Council, and the Manitoba Government for our publishing program.

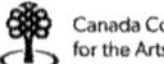

Canada Council for the Arts Conseil des arts du Canada Funded by the Government of Canada Canada Manitoba Arts Council Conseil des arts du Manitoba

J. Gordon Shillingford Publishing
P.O. Box 86, RPO Corydon Avenue, Winnipeg, MB Canada R3M 3S3

To Black immigrant women—to your bodies—and the traumas you have suffered in the name of your children. To Sheryl, Magdalene and Sandra.

Kanika Ambrose

Kanika Ambrose is a playwright, librettist and screenwriter. Her play *our place* was first produced by Cahoots Theatre and Theatre Passe Muraille in November 2022 and received a Dora Mavor Moore Award for Outstanding New Play in June 2023. She is a graduate of Canadian Film Centre's Bell Media Primetime TV Program (2022–2023). Her children's opera *Anansi and the Great Light* (with composer Nick diBerardino and the students at Girard College) premiered at Curtis Institute of Music (Philadelphia) in 2019. Her opera *Of the Sea* (with composer Ian Cusson) premiered at the Bluma Appel Theatre in March 2023, commissioned by Tapestry Opera and Obsidian Theatre Company. Other short works have premiered across North America including celebrated digital work *Tak-Tak-Shoo* (with composer Rene Orth). Kanika is a graduate of Toronto Metropolitan University and is Associate Artistic Director of Necessary Angel Theatre Company. She was featured as one of Cahoots Theatre Company's "30 for 30" theatre makers for their 30th anniversary season. A long-time Scarborough native, Kanika currently lives in Orono, Ontario with her husband and two-year-old son.

Acknowledgements

This play would not have been possible without the early and ongoing support of Cahoots Theatre, including two cohorts of their Hot House Program and another as OAC Playwright in Residence. To that end I would like to thank: Alicia Richardson, Amanda Cordner, Amanda Parris, Andrea Scott, Brefny Caribou, Derek Kwan, En Lai Mah, Flerida Peña, Jake Runeckles, Jasmine Chen, Jessica Watkin, Jo SiMalaya Alcampo, Keshia Palm, Kevin Matthew Wong, Kirsten Kirsch, Raf Antonio, Shiasta Latif, Suvendrini Lena, Tsholo Khalema. The artists involved in workshops and readings: Jamie Robinson, Marcel Stewart, Joella Crichton, Araya Mengesha, Marc Senior, Peter Bailey, Kaleb Alexander, Allison Edwards Crewe, Sodienye Waboso Amajor, Emerjade Simms. Special thanks to Virgilia Griffith, Sophia Walker and Sabryn Rock for sticking with me through many workshops, cancellations and COVID, with love, grace and enthusiasm. And to Tremaine Nelson and Pablo Ogunlesi for completing that incredible first cast.

Thank you to the Toronto Arts Council, Ontario Arts Council and Canada Council for the Arts for your support at all stages.

Thank you to my husband, whose stories helped inspire this work.

Thank you to all of Cahoots' leadership teams who supported my work over the years; Kat Horzema, Kat Ann Vandemeer, Sehar Bhojani, Indrit Kasapi and to Marjorie Chan, who, when all I had was two characters in two scenes, saw the value in this story and saw that it was, in fact, a play. Thank you to Tanisha Taitt, Lisa Alves and Samantha Vu, who worked tirelessly to see this play through to the best first production I could have ever asked for.

Playwright's Note

There's been talk, for a long time, in Caribbean Canadian communities, about the challenges of immigrating to Canada without certain programs to fast-track their admission. In 2016, these conversations were heightened when there was a war in the world and 25,000 people were flown into Canada. These conversations were difficult to hear; I was angry and ashamed that people in my community were having them. Upon my investigation of that shame of people I love, I realized that, as with many things, this was caused by the pressures of a broken system.

The Canadian immigration system is broken — on so many levels. It has been broken since the inception of this country as we know it, but, looking at what it is today, it's no wonder people are frustrated. And people who are frustrated and in the midst of grappling with their own survival struggle sometimes lose the capacity for the empathy that those of us with secure housing, work, and food supplies are able to have.

There are people who have been waiting on word for visa and immigration applications for close to a decade. There are people who entered the country by other means and, years later, still cannot secure safe housing. There are people who are in all kinds of (often exploitative) arrangements in order to survive while keeping under the government's radar.

It's different than a war, but it is a different war. For the record, I want everyone to have what they need. I want all people to be safe in their homes; those are basic needs that should be met for everyone. I am also sure that the people I heard having troublesome conversations surrounding the war want those things, too. I truly believe that there aren't many people who want ugly things to happen to other people, but chaotic systems create chaos, and ruthless, unfeeling systems support the development of ruthless sentiments. It's sad, it's true, and it's all around.

Kanika Ambrose
(Playwright's note from the program of the original production.)

Foreword

I had the pleasure of first really encountering Kanika at the Fringe Festival of Toronto where she was performing her show *The Art of Traditional Head-Tying* (2014). I was enthralled by her delightful characterizations and her capacity to capture the humanity and humour of Dominica, her family's home in the Caribbean. I waited after the show in order to congratulate and perhaps get to know Kanika a little better. There was also another woman waiting, and she stayed largely silent as I raved with enthusiastic musings about Kanika's show. Perhaps in hindsight, there was a definitely a twinkle in her eye. When Kanika came outside, I learned I was waiting with Kanika's mother, who had said nary a word as I gushed. We all shared a laugh. It was a lovely first connection.

Over the years, I certainly did get to know Kanika better, as she joined the development unit at Cahoots Theatre (where I previously was Artistic Director). Then, as she continued to write and create, I had the privilege of encountering her other works, filled with her emotional clarity, and gifted with rich stories. And then most recently, I was witness to her process as *our place* was produced at Theatre Passe Muraille (alongside producing partner Cahoots Theatre). Little has changed since that Fringe show; I continue to be awed by her talent, composure and absolute consummate storytelling. There is an immense quiet confidence to her work. She knows the story she wants to tell and how she wants to tell it. I gushed again to Kanika's mother on the opening night of *our place,* this time knowingly. I hope this will be the beginning of many, many more opening nights.

In Kanika's poignant and timely script, she deftly unpacks the lives of two women, undocumented and living in Canada, against the backdrop of a Scarborough jerk restaurant. Scarborough, as a part of Toronto, is often upheld for its cultural diversity and breadth of representation from around the globe. As an example, my immigrant family also sought out the cultural plurality of Scarborough to raise my sister and me. Further, Scarborough is often looked to as an emblem of Canada itself — a welcoming, benevolent country that opens its arms to the world and embraces everyone. We are treated to photos of a beaming prime minister greeting families at the airport, or the smiles of newly arrived immigrants at their first hockey game in attempts to foster a nationalistic pride in how we, as a country, *welcome*. To be certain, many times, Canada has been a beacon of hope for many.

These engaging photogenic opportunities belie the immense complexity that is Canadian immigration, as well as diminish the circumstances of those attempting to achieve the "Canadian dream." For those with limited means and channels, their choices are slim and often individuals must take enormous risks in trying to achieve citizenship.

Kanika has skillfully created the world of *our place* in order to question and examine our complicity in this inequitable system through a humorous and compassionate lens. With sensitivity, we follow two young women through their joy, their vulnerabilities and their decision-making. Here in Toronto, ostensibly a sanctuary city, these women represent many, many other undocumented people. And this is a story that is replicated in many major cities. Kanika shares this story so brilliantly through her play. I feel deeply in love with the characters, through their foibles, successes and difficult decisions. I laughed with them, and I cried with them and ultimately, I felt that through Kanika's portraits I knew them.

Enjoy.

Marjorie Chan
Toronto, June 2023

Note on Text

*** is a beat filled with the strong transmission of some kind of strong feeling from one character to another, usually disgust, incredulity, or a combination of both. The more asterisks, the more disgust, incredulity, rage, etc… the character transmits. It can also just be confusion or actively waiting for the other character to respond.

/ is where the character with the next line should begin speaking.

— is an interruption. The character can interrupt their own thought or be interrupted by someone else.

Note on Dialect

Fanon and Caviva are fictional islands created by the playwright. As such, the dialects have also been constructed. Fanonian is written in Dominican (Commonwealth of Dominica) dialect and blended with some Haitian sounds and Creole.

Cavivan is written in Jamaican dialect but with Guyanese sounds. These dialects were created in collaboration with Alicia Richardson. Future productions should contact Alicia for use of her resource kit on these dialects: Alicia.dionne.richardson@gmail.com.

On the topic of fiction, Jerk Pork Castle is also not real… don't feel bad if you didn't know about it.

Note on Music

The music is as fictious as the dialects. I was thinking dancehall mashup for Caviva and Bouyon/Zouk mashup for Fanon._

Future productions should contact DJ L'Oqenz, the original Sound Designer/Composer, for use of her original compositions, c/o Dave Guenette daveg@piratesblend.com

For Future Productions

I suggest the use of these created nationalities, dialects and music in future productions, however, if there is a strong demographic of two particular Caribbean groups in the region where the play is being produced, the production may choose to have the character's nationalities and dialects reflect those communities.

Similarly, it may make sense to change the locations that are specific to Scarborough to a similar region local to your production, i.e. "Thompson Park" can be another park suitable for large community festivals. "Kingston Road" can be any street where there is a high immigrant population. Scarborough itself can be replaced by another area that is a subset of a larger city and is a place of great diversity of culture and income.

Glossary

Listen, a glossary for this play might as well include every single word. If you don't know what something says and I didn't translate it in brackets, try saying it out loud. If it sounds like something familiar, that's probably what it is and if you still don't know, the whole sentence should "help yuh tuh tek de sense in it!" Oh ya, Cavivians drop the "h" at the front of words so that sentence should read… " 'elp yuh tuh tek de sense in it." Undastan'?"

Here's a few terms that might help you a bit:

Fanonian:	**Cavivian:**
In general, "D" or "F" replace "TH" – Dat = That, Dere/Dyah = There, De/Der = The, Fink = Think Long "ee" words are shortened with an "i." Like "Street" is "Strit." "Need" is "Nid." *In both dialects, some of the characters code switch. Pay attention to when this happens and why. * There are exceptions to every rule. That's what makes it fun.	In general, "H" as the first or second letter in a word is dropped so "Harvey would be "'arvey," "Think" would be "Tink." Same with "W" words so "who" would be "ooo" Mi = I or I'm Ar = Or Guh = Go Fi/Fuh = For or To Some "o" sounds are written with an "a." "College" is written/pronounced as "Callege," "Worker" is "Warka."

Historical Context

As Scene 1 suggests, the play takes place in 2016 after the Canadian government "resettled" 25,000 Syrian refugees. (The term "resettled" is the government's.) There was also a backlog in processing for some of the other immigration programs. I encourage anyone who's interested to have a look at Canada.ca/en/services/immigration/citizenship. Immigration policy updates all the time; the current policies are there and there are also archives which lead to what they were at the time of this play and beyond.

Production History

our place was first performed at Theatre Passe Muraille, Toronto, Ontario, November 18–December 3, 2022, a co-production of Cahoots Theatre and Theatre Passe Muraille.

Cast

Andrea: .... Virgilia Griffith

Niesha: .... Sophia Walker

Malcolm: .... Tremaine Nelson

Eldrick: .... Pablo Ogunlisi

Creative Team

Playwright: .... Kanika Ambrose

Director: .... Sabryn Rock

Producer: .... Lisa Alves

Stage Manager: .... Jennifer Stobart

ASM: .... Reva Lokhande

Set and Costumes Designer: .... Sim Suzer

Lighting Designer: .... Shawn Henry

Video Designer: .... Shayne Levine

Sound Designer: .... NON

Associate Producer:............................. Samantha Vu

Production Supervisor:....................... Rebecca Vandevelde

Production Manager: .... Maya Royer

Rehearsal Stage Manager: .... Emilie Aubin

Rehearsal ASM:................................... Wei Qing Tan

Head of Props: .... Chynah Philadelphia

Set and Costume Design Mentor: .... Joanna Yu

Dialect Coach: .... Alicia Richardson

Intimacy Coordinator: .... Anita Nittoly

Niesha (Sophia Walker) begs Andrea (Virgilia Griffith) to help her learn to lure Eldrick. Cahoots Theatre / Theatre Passe Muraille Production, 2022. Photo by Gesilayefa Azorbo.

Eldrick (Pablo Ogunlisi) and Malcolm (Tremaine Nelson) are reunited for the first time in years at Jerk Pork Castle, preventing the women from closing the shop. Cahoots Theatre / Theatre Passe Muraille Production, 2022. Photo by Gesilayefa Azorbo

Andrea (Virgilia Griffith) greets Malcolm (Tremaine Nelson); showing off her new outfit. Cahoots Theatre/Theatre Passe Muraille Production, 2022. Photo by Gesilayefa Azorbo.

Niesha (Sophia Walker) recounts to Eldrick (Pablo Ogunlesi) the moment she knew she had to go through with marrying him. Cahoots Theatre/Theatre Passe Muraille Production, 2022. Photo by Gesilayefa Azorbo.

Characters

ANDREA: .... Early 30s, Black, works at Jerk Pork Castle, from the island Caviva.

NIESHA: .... Late 30s, Black, works at Jerk Pork Castle, from the island Fanon.

MALCOLM: .... Late 30s, Black, Canadian originally from Caviva. Came to Canada as a child.

ELDRICK: .... 30, Black, Canadian originally from Fanon.

Setting

Act 1 takes place in various locations in Scarborough, with the main hub being a small storefront Caribbean restaurant called Jerk Pork Castle. If you don't know about it, you better be about it and ask about it! Three square bistro tables with chairs and a booth with barstools. Food is showcased in a glass warmer case next to the cash register. It's a typical small Scarborough, Caribbean restaurant layout.

Act 2: a hotel room in Niagara Falls. A queen bed, night table, breakfast table, dresser, TV, bathroom. That's it. Shouldn't have cost them more than $35 a night on Trivago. Okay, let's go!

Prelude

North Scarborough. Think Neilson and Sewells. A house party. An ol'skool Cavivan tune plays. Enter ANDREA, dressed better than the dancehall queen; something tight, bright and neon. She begins to dance.

Niagara Falls. A hotel room. Think $34/night on Groupon. NIESHA in cheap lingerie. Think something you would try to bargain down at the flea market. ELDRICK in his underwear. Fruit of the Loom. They sit on the bed. NIESHA on the phone. ELDRICK waiting for her to hang up.

Party. MALCOLM enters, sees ANDREA and begins to compete with her in a dance-off.

Niagara Falls. NIESHA shoves the box of food away from her.

House Party. MALCOLM and ANDREA are now dancing together. She's bubbling her waist; he's whining on her boomsie. It's hot.

ELDRICK and NIESHA are in the bed. NIESHA is off the phone and giving him her full attention. He slips one strap off her lingerie…or something.

MALCOLM and ANDREA agree to leave together.

ACT ONE

Scene 1

Jerk Pork Castle. Scarborough. A little further south. Somewhere along Kingston Road east of Galloway.

8:40 pm. NIESHA is wiping down the tables with a damp cloth. ANDREA is combing her hair back into a ponytail, wiping the counter, eating a plate of leftover food, cleaning the kitchen and dancing to the same Cavivan tune from the party. The TV mounted above the window is on CP24; NIESHA watches the news while she works.

NIESHA turns up the TV, ANDREA turns up the music, NIESHA turns up the TV, ANDREA turns up the music, NIESHA turns up the TV.

ANDREA: Turn dat aff man, shite!

NIESHA: Am watchin' it.

ANDREA: Mi say, turn it aff, tantie (aunty)!

NIESHA: An' I say watch am watchin' it. I nid to hear my news. Ou konprann (you understand)?

ANDREA kisses her teeth

ANDREA: You don' see me a try listen tuh my music?

NIESHA: When we leave dere in twenty minutes, you can listen to your music all night to your heart content.

ANDREA: You 'ave da ol' TV on one channel alone all dyay—

NIESHA: De clients like it.

ANDREA: —an' iz one fing ova an' ova 'bout Syria, Syria, Syria, for da pass' six-seven monts. Dem nah a'ready brin' twenty-five tousan' a' dem? An' dem still wan' brin' more?

NIESHA: Yes, an' dat good for dem.

ANDREA: 'oo say suh? If dis ere gov'ment wan tek een so much a' dem, wha' yuh tink guh 'appen tuh us? Crack downk (down)!

NIESHA: I don' know what you talkin' dere.

ANDREA: 'Ow yuh mean? Yuh tink sey dey a' mek we stay 'ere?

NIESHA: Shh!

ANDREA: Yuh tink dey care two ras about us?

NIESHA: I say low down your voice!

ANDREA: Fuh wha'?

NIESHA: Andrea, I don' have time— Why I always have tuh tell you—

ANDREA: Easy Niesha; nobady di' dere wid us.

NIESHA: Anybody could come inside de shop any minute; iz a public / restaurant.

ANDREA: / Yuh tink sey I care ooo 'ear me? A true me talk!

NIESHA: Just because is de troof (truth) you haven' got to shout it out over de mountaintops, eh eh! An' you haven' got a right to talk my troof an' your troof as if is de same fing! Aye bondjay (my god)—you want to shout? Shout about yuh ownself, but don' tie me up in your nonsense!

ANDREA kisses her teeth.

ANDREA: Awl talk more quiet. Only out of respec for mi eldars.

She lowers her tone.

Bettar?

Beat.

NIESHA: We' closin' dere too early. If Yvonne come dere she'll have wuds (words) for us.

ANDREA: Yvonne only come 'round 'ere on shipment d'yay.

NIESHA: You neva know—

ANDREA: An' she only start do dat when she smart up an' realize sey some a 'er ol' employees—not nyamin' (naming) nyames—wuh dere 'elping demselves to whole box a' meat.

NIESHA: Wicked set a' people.

ANDREA: Mi seh, mi not a teef (thief), but mi nah believe sey dis rest'rant 'ere sell off 'all de meat it buy up. Yvonne prob'ly come 'ere on shipment dyay fi 'elp 'erself tuh.

NIESHA: So, you callin' Yvonne a feef?

ANDREA: Well…

NIESHA: Rememba, she doin' us a big favour an' takin' a big risk. You mus have more respec'.

ANDREA: Joke mi mek! Mi cyan'na (cannot) mek a likkle joke? Yuh suh bahrin'(boring); yuh neva wan' she tuh 'ave fun!

NIESHA: Not while at work.

ANDREA: 'Ow come mi get so much shifs wid you? Prefer a' work wid Dawnnie.

NIESHA: Because boaf of you all lazy.

ANDREA: All yuh wan fi do is watch de stchu'pid news! Man! Dis 'ere refugee ting rel'ly cheese me up, fuh so.

NIESHA: Why you mek it boda (bother) you so?

ANDREA: Why yuh nah mek it bah'dda yuh? Check dis; yuh an' I leave ar countries—

NIESHA: You an'? —

ANDREA: Sarry— I lef my dear country, sweet Cavivuh— don' know 'bout you. Don' know where yuh even come from—

NIESHA: Fanon.

ANDREA: Right— I lef my country, Cavivuh, tuh try fine a betta life for me an' mi chil'ren.

Inna my country, I don' 'ave no jahb (job)— mos' a di people dem nah 'ave no jahb. Vi'lence every dyay, lots a' people a' loot an' steal, 'specially afta da 'urricyane! Not a lot of educyational oppa'tunity. I fear for my life—an' for da life of mi chil'ren.

NIESHA: By all accounts, iz you dat take your chance an come here illegal.

ANDREA: By all account, I 'ave all da criteria tuh be a refugee!

NIESHA: You had a choice, refugees do not.

ANDREA: Now yuh talk like dem—Yuh wan' talk like dem e? Ooo decide ooo dere pon refugee an ooo just illegal? Some group a' white man? B'caw dem write it down on a piece a p'yaypa (paper), dat mek it true? Dem mek up de rules fi suit ooo ever sey dem wan'—Mi nah know 'bout you, but, even doe mi nah come from no war tarn county, mi didn' choose to come 'ere illegahl.

NIESHA: Andrea, you' pushin' it.

ANDREA: Trus' me, if dere was a legahl option for me I would'a tek it lang time ago, but from us—

NIESHA: Us—?

ANDREA: *(She indicates her skin colour.)* Us. —dem only wan' skill worker; callege, university degree, Bachelars an' Mastars an' Doctars in de Arts, people like dat are of value! Not dose of us who spen' so much a wi time ben' downk (down) a wash toilet an scrub up floor dat if dere was a degree in dat!

NIESHA: Why you don' go ahead and scream it out in de strits, nah!

ANDREA: An' a fry up chickeen in 'ot burnin ail (oil)!

NIESHA: Wait. Lemme open up de front door for you.

NIESHA walks to the front door.

ANDREA: An' chyangin' pee-pee sheet. Bai (boy), if dem 'ave degree in dat!

NIESHA: Look—

ANDREA: If dem eva mek degree in dat I woulda did 'ave mi Ph.D.!

NIESHA: Look! I open de door. If iz audience you want, you have whole of Kingston Road.

ANDREA: So we didn' 'ave no odda (other) choice but tuh look 'bout w'yay mek we enta true da back door. Mek yuh close da door now, I finish.

NIESHA: Sure?

ANDREA: Yeh, Mammy, shut up da place.

NIESHA shuts the door.

NIESHA: Girl, sometimes your mouf jus' talk a pile of nonsense!

ANDREA: Nansense mi talk deh? Hmp! If iz talk mi talk nansense den tell me ooo talkin troot?

We mus' fi get creative, mi say, 'bout findin our w'yays in. An' if dere's one ting I am extremely good in, it's creativity.

Beat.

Ken you 'urry up an' finish wid dose tyables? Mi av' fi mop da floors so we can leave.

NIESHA: De shop don' closin' yet.

ANDREA: So wha'? Yuh tink anybady a' come 'ere fifteen minutes before wi lack.

NIESHA: So wut you rushin' for?

ANDREA: I 'ave a date wit Malcolm, abviously.

NIESHA: How you mean obviously? I supposed to know all of what goes on in your life?

ANDREA: Well abviously if mi pull out dese pant.

She pulls out her outfit from a bag behind the counter.

An dis tap. An' dese 'ere shoe. Ah' mus' be goin' out wid someone special.

NIESHA: Hmp! Dose are reeeelly somefing.

ANDREA: Tanks.

ANDREA goes into the kitchen to change behind the fridge.

Mi buy dem up a' Pickering Flea Market. Mi check sey, Malcolm an' I been dealin' a'ready ova five mont an' 'im see all mi odda outfit a'ready. Mi 'ave ta fresh up mi bag a' tricks, seen? 'ave to keep 'im interested!

NIESHA: You all been checkin' five monf already? You only been here for six!

ANDREA: Girl, b'fore mi set foot on plane mi know sey where da party guh be, wha kine a' man guh reach an' wha kine a ooman 'im like. Mi nah come 'ere fi play; mi a'fi get my man an' mek it so sweet 'im a'fi beg me fi stay! Bai, mi nah mess aroun'k; mi nah fi go back a' Cavivuh.

Beat. ANDREA emerges from the kitchen; dressed to the nines.

'Ow mi look?

NIESHA: Iz a likkle much.

ANDREA: Tanks. Moonlight Lounge 'ave a dance, den mi tink sey we prob'bly go down to da bluffs an'…

NIESHA: An'… watch yuhself, eh.

ANDREA: Me? Nobady more careful dan mi!

NIESHA: You don' tol him nuffin?

ANDREA: Nat yet.

NIESHA: You plannin' to?

ANDREA: No! don' tink awl need tuh.

NIESHA: He don' axe you where you livin', den? Your chil'ren?

ANDREA: We nah really in'tuh conversyation.

NIESHA: Good. Bes' keep it like dat.

ANDREA: Ooh! Watchya! You fas'!

NIESHA: Becaw sometimes you tell people your situation an' dey does preten dey want to gi you a help, or even dey do want tuh help you, for true, but word get aroung to de wrong person or dey demself is de wrong person and iz— iz just a big problem for you.

ANDREA: Dat man don' know nuttin 'bout me 'cept where tuh guh get it!

They laugh a little.

NIESHA: Young girl, you trouble, you know!

ANDREA: Where you turnin' out tuhnight?

NIESHA: *(Teasing.)* Me? I don' know.

ANDREA: Ooohhhh?!

NIESHA: After I close up de shop—

ANDREA: Mmm hmm?

NIESHA: I gettin' on de express bus, route D—

ANDREA: Yeeeeaaa?!

NIESHA: Go home—

ANDREA: Get dressed? Go out?

NIESHA: Awa. Jus' go home, nuh? Lie down on de couch an' call my chir'ren.

ANDREA: Continuin' your legacy as da mos' bahrin' oooman in da 'ole a' Scarborough.

NIESHA: Abigail had debate in school today; I mus' call her and hear how it go an wedda Sammy drivin' my sister mad as yet. He come so troublesome!

ANDREA: Mi know say wha' yuh talk, Benjamin's a likkle 'andful (handful) tuh.

A knock on the window.

Oooo! Dere's Malcolm.

NIESHA: *(Under her breath.)* Hooray.

ANDREA opens the door for MALCOLM.

ANDREA: Wha'am b'yaby! (What's happening baby)

MALCOLM: Hey.

She throws her arms around him. A long kiss.

ANDREA: All day mi min' deh pan yuh. (my mind was on you)

MALCOLM: I missed you too.

ANDREA: Did yuh 'ad a nice day?

MALCOLM: Long an' dread as usual.

ANDREA: Don' worry 'bout dat now. Look.

She stands back and models her new outfit for MALCOLM.

MALCOLM: Oh wow. Nice!

ANDREA: Oh! Wait!

She grabs earrings from her bag and puts them on.

Now?

MALCOLM: Even better.

ANDREA: Yuh like it?

MALCOLM: Well, yeah.

Another long gropey kiss.

You ready to go?

ANDREA: Almos', mi jus' need Niesha tuh finish wipe up da tyables fi mi tuh map up da floor — Niesha, yuh almos' finish?

NIESHA: Yep.

MALCOLM: Hi, Niesha.

NIESHA: Know what Ani, why you don' go out an' enjoy you' allself an' I will pass a mop on de floor before I leave.

ANDREA: No, I wouldn't mek yuh do dat.

ANDREA sprays perfume under her armpits.

NIESHA: It not even takin' me ten minutes. De place not so big.

ANDREA: Yes, but it'a my jab (job).

NIESHA: Iz not somefing you do all da time. An' you relly lookin' nice.

MALCOLM: You sure? You don't want me to drop you somewhere?

NIESHA: No—

ANDREA: She prab'bly 'ave a 'ot date 'erself.

MALCOLM: Wid who?

NIESHA: Uh uh—

ANDREA: And she wan' we fi lef 'er alone so we don' see.

NIESHA: Awa (oh no)— can you all jus' go so I can finish tidyin' up for me to leave also?

I wan' for me to catch de ten twenty-seven bus for me to get home an' stretch my foot.

ANDREA: Okay. Finish up suh you can get 'ome tuh brown couch.

NIESHA: Brown couch betta dan carpet on floor.

ANDREA: *(Aside, to NIESHA.)* Ey, ooo knows, maybe mi a lay p'on king size bed tuhnight!

Enter ELDRICK.

ELDRICK: Evenin'.

MALCOLM: Ey! Wha' happening, bred?

ELDRICK: Ey! Wadup, padna (partner)?

NIESHA: *(Aside, to ANDREA.)* Nobody goin' an' come fifteen minutes to close eh?

MALCOLM: Haven't seen you in a minute still! You don't live round here again?

ELDRICK: Nah, mans all the way up Markham way. Up past Steeles.

MALCOLM: Up north, eh? Scene?

ELDRICK: Ya, I was just down here checkin' a scene and mans got ma'ved, you know? (marved = Scarborough for extremely hungry)

MALCOLM: I hear you, still. I don' know how much food's lef', dough (though); they're almost close.

But yo, I'm sure Niesha can fix you up, still.

ELDRICK: Yuh check?

MALCOLM: Yo Niesha! Fix up my bredren iight? Long time he haven't taste some Kingston Road jerk chicken!

ELDRICK: Alright, padna (partner); we should link up.

MALCOLM: Scene. You know where mans be. Just come through here and axe Andrea ar Niesha; eider one a dem can tell you where I stay.

ELDRICK: Andrea, pleasure to meet you.

ANDREA holds out her hand. ELDRICK shakes it.

ANDREA: Ani.

ELDRICK: JPC's re'lly upgraded dere employees… new uniform?

ANDREA: Lot a Caribbean rest'rant on a dis 'ere street; Yvonne 'ad fi do wha' she could tuh keep customers int'rested.

ELDRICK: I'll be comin' back for sure.

MALCOLM: Alright man, we're just headin' out but definitely link me next time ur coming true (through).

ELDRICK: Ya man, no doubt.

ANDREA: Bye, Niesha. Yuh okay by yourself?

NIESHA: Clearly am not by myself.

ANDREA: *(To ELDRICK.)* Jus' tek ur chicken an' guh lang let Niesha lack up da shop. She not sayin', but mi know sey she 'ave big plan tuhnight!

Exit MALCOLM and ANDREA, groping, kissing. ELDRICK stays.

Shift. NIESHA finishes the tables and grabs a mop and bucket to wash the floor. She turns the TV up even louder.

ELDRICK: You ain't get da new uniform?

NIESHA: Not my size.

ELDRICK: Or you ain't got no fancy car padna' pickin' you up tonight?

NIESHA: None of your business.

ELDRICK: So, what food you got dere?

NIESHA: Dere close.

ELDRICK: Door was unlock when I came in.

NIESHA: Still close.

ELDRICK: Says you closin' at nine.

NIESHA: Yep. Iz now nine o' two.

ELDRICK: I been here more dan two minutes.

NIESHA: Den you stan' up dere, run your mouf, flirt wiv woman an' de time pass.

ELDRICK: Come on. Dat is a bit mean. Am sure Yvonne would not like to know you dere running off her customers.

NIESHA: How you know Yvonne?

ELDRICK: Did some work on de restaurant some time a back. Tiling, countertop, likkle fing here an' dere. Used to live down de strit in dose brown apartment buildin's.

NIESHA: Dere's always trouble at dose buildin's dere.

ELDRICK: Dat is de reason I leave.

NIESHA: Fanon you come from, man?

ELDRICK: Yeh. You could tell, eh?

NIESHA: Yeh. De accent a bit fade out but…

ELDRICK: Li la toujou (it's still there).

NIESHA: Well, we out of food, so we close.

ELDRICK: Dere's food right dere on der (the) counter.

NIESHA: Dat's mines.

ELDRICK: Souple Cherie (please sweetie); I don' need too much.

NIESHA: Iz been sittin' out all day.

ELDRICK: Ba mwen yon ti tak (give me a little bit).

NIESHA: Dat sure upset your stomach. Yvonne wouldn't want me to give out food dat make customers sick.

ELDRICK: Why iz good for your stomach but not good for mines?

NIESHA puts down the mop and bucket and gets behind the counter.

NIESHA: What can I get you?

ELDRICK: Hold— am just goin to have a look at der board.

NIESHA: Don' bodda; not one fing dere is correc.

ELDRICK: Not one fing?

NIESHA: Well, seein' as we close, we don' have none a' dat lef.

Comes out from behind the counter and looks at the board.

NIESHA: Yep. All dat incorrec. All we have is what you see in front of you.

ELDRICK: Cool. Lemme see...

NIESHA: Dere have piece jerk chicken, yon ti kal (a little bit) curry goat, jerk pork, plain rice, an' a likkle bit a green salad, petit, petit (small)...

ELDRICK: Dat plenty!

NIESHA: Scraps.

ELDRICK: Like I say'd, I don' eat much.

NIESHA: I don' have gravy, eh.

ELDRICK: No gravy at all?

NIESHA: Dere have a bit a' oxtail gravy in a pot—

ELDRICK: So, bring it come.

NIESHA: But I don' have no oxtail.

ELDRICK: Matters not.

She looks at him with disgust.

I'll have der jerk pork.

NIESHA: Jerk pork wif oxtail gravy an' no oxtail?

ELDRICK: Right.

NIESHA: ********

Rice?

ELDRICK: Yes.

NIESHA: Salad?

ELDRICK: Please. Give me der balance of der curry goat as well.

NIESHA: Nope! One meat. Two meat, two separate meal.

ELDRICK: Come on! I'm your last customer for de night.

NIESHA: Is a different price.

ELDRICK: I just want a likkle piece and you can take de rest home if you want.

NIESHA: No. Not to worry. Just take all of it.

She piles all of the food into a container and pushes it toward him.

ELDRICK: Fank you.

NIESHA: Yeh.

ELDRICK: Tie it in a plastic for me.

NIESHA: **

ELDRICK: I don' want for it to drip.

NIESHA goes to get a white plastic bag in the back.

You're new dere?

NIESHA: Kind of.

ELDRICK: How long you been workin' at JPC?

She comes back with the bag and packs up the food.

NIESHA: Long enough.

ELDRICK: How long is dat?

NIESHA: How long since you move?

ELDRICK: Why you can never give a straight answer? You always have some roundabout answer to every fing I axe.

NIESHA: Maybe 'cause you axein' me de wrong questions. Maybe if you axe me how much you owe me for de food you come for, I givin' you an answer rel straight.

ELDRICK: How much I owe you for de food?

NIESHA: Eleven ninety-five.

ELDRICK: I only have ten.

NIESHA: Den you only will stay hungry.

ELDRICK gives her $15.00. She gives him back change.

ELDRICK: You're cute.

NIESHA: You're young. Nid napkin?

ELDRICK: Frow some in de bag, nuh. You have boyfren?

NIESHA: Foak an' knife?

ELDRICK: I'll take dat as a no. Lucky me. Am Eldrick, by der way.

He holds out his hand for a handshake.

NIESHA: **

ELDRICK: And you are Niesha. Pleased to make your acquaintances.

NIESHA: **

ELDRICK: Fanks for der food.

NIESHA: Neva'mine.

ELDRICK: How you gettin' home? I can give you a ride somewhere?

NIESHA: Yuh fink iz stupid I stupid to go in car wif strange man I just mit? Bus.

ELDRICK: Whereabouts are you located?

NIESHA: Bus.

ELDRICK: Suit yourself—Oh! — (Kisses teeth.) I need a pop.

NIESHA: Which one?

ELDRICK: Root beer.

NIESHA: Dolla.

She hands him the root beer. He hands her the dollar. Lingers a minute.

ELDRICK: I'll see you aroung.

NIESHA: Where?

ELDRICK: Here. Am finking of stoppin' 'roung here more often. I like de company.

NIESHA: Wavo (bravo)!

ELDRICK: Maybe sometime I'll leave wif more dan just a container of food.

NIESHA: We don' have noffin' else sellin' dere but food.

ELDRICK: What I want, money cannot buy

NIESHA: I have yet to find noffin' dat come for free.

ELDRICK: Good night, Niesha.

NIESHA finishes cleaning the restaurant; packs up her bag and leaves.

Scene 2

Bluffers Park. The back seat of a Toyota RAV4. MALCOLM and ANDREA are making out in the back. A slow jam plays on the system.

ANDREA: 'Ey.

MALCOLM: Mm.

ANDREA: 'Eeeyyyy!

MALCOLM: Mmhmm?

ANDREA pushes MALCOLM away. He sits up.

What's up?

ANDREA: Mi wah tinkin' earlier; mi a you been datin' a few mont an' it 'ould be nice tuh guh out on a rel dyate.

MALCOLM: Like what?

ANDREA: A dyate, dyate.

MALCOLM: What are we doing now? We didn't just come here and do dis. We pass through Twilight… had two drink.

ANDREA: Yeh, an' it was gud. But mi tink sey we could do someting new. Like some people go out for dinnar ar a movie.

MALCOLM: Uh huh.

ANDREA: Ar even da same ting; walk in da park in da dyay time.

MALCOLM: I work in the daytime; so do you.

ANDREA: M'know. Mi nah axin' fi all da time. Just once in a while.

MALCOLM: Okay... so you wanna go on a date. Okay, so… you're an amazing dancer, you like shopping…

ANDREA: Liam Neeson movie…

MALCOLM: Yes! How could I forget that? Liam Neeson movies…fuckin' weird—

ANDREA: 'Im bod! Why 'im weird?

MALCOLM: He's not weird; you just... won't watch a movie unless he's in it... which is weird. Anywayz—what other kinda tings you like to do? You into the live music tings?

ANDREA: Mi nah know. Mi spen so much time a work mi nah relly get to explore mi intres's. Mi tink sey mi always di like nature. Yeh, like anytime mi guh round trees an' farest an' garden, mi mine' always jus' free up. Like mi nah 'ave nah badda nah stress. But mi neva get ta visit dem type a places alat.

MALCOLM: Scene, scene. I like the nature ting too, still.

ANDREA: Ya?

MALCOLM: Ya, like not like hiking or camping or none a dat, but I do go down a Thompson Park for Ribfest two time.

ANDREA: Mi love rib!

MALCOLM: I do know dere are some nice places aroun' here and maybe you and me can explore dem together, yuh nuh? When's your nex' day off?

ANDREA: Sunday.

MALCOLM: We'll check out the Botanical Gardens on Sunday den.

ANDREA: Sound gud.

MALCOLM: Why didn't you tell me you had a problem with dis before? It's always kinda just been our ting. We party, den chill. Go back to my place or the bluffs, drink, talk shit, den vibe; we have a good time. You kinda, never really had a problem wid it.

ANDREA: Mi neva say dere was a problem. Mi jus' want me a' you relationship tuh guh lang strong, yuh know? Mi wan' fi get tuh know you bettar—wha' yuh like—

MALCOLM: You know what I like.

ANDREA: Serious! Mi don' wan' yuh fi jus' wan' me for a gud time, scene?

MALCOLM: Andrea I'm not dat kind of guy. I thought we had an understanding and both of us were cool— but if dis isn't what you want—

ANDREA: No, no, mi definitely wan' dis.

She puts his hand back on her body.

I wuh jus' tinkin' e' might be gud.

MALCOLM starts to lower himself on top of her.

MALCOLM: It might be good.

ANDREA: E' might be gud tuh—

MALCOLM: Might be—

They kiss.

Shift. NIESHA at home, on the phone.

NIESHA: Sammy? Yes, baby, I know you relly want a pair of Claks but Mammy cannot get you everyfing you want. Abby out of de bafroom yet? Go an call her, nuh; Tell her Mammy's on de phone an' want to hear how her debate go. Not to tell me for you to spoil it! Yes, my son, love you too. Abby!

Scene 3

Jerk Pork Castle. Two weeks later. ANDREA has just come in and is changing into her uniform. NIESHA is at the back, prepping food, hidden by the fridge. She can appear and disappear as needed.

ANDREA on the phone reading off a Western Union confirmation sheet.

ANDREA: Aylen, listen mi tell yuh, da confarmation numbah be 3467910024. Use da same address I gi' yuh da las' time fi Dawnnie Nelson. Use 'im address cuz yuh know yuh cyan' use mines. Ah tryin mi' bes,' Aylen—barrow da money tuh pay da light bill, an de chicken. Trus' whateva' yuh 'ave tuh—some neighba mus' be able tuh help a likkle langa (longer). Ah pramise am workin' an it—ah be so close!... Put my baby an da phone. Le Ann, Alicia, whichever one di dere. Dey nat dere? —okay, will talk tuh dem lata. Yeh man! Nuh problem.

Beat.

NIESHA: Everything okay?

ANDREA: Yeh, man mammie— Mi see mi mus get a new dress.

NIESHA: How comes?

ANDREA: Malcolm guh tek me tuh Taranto Islands!

NIESHA: Wow. Malcolm steppin' up. Last week it was—

ANDREA: Botanical Gardens.

NIESHA: An' now you goin' on boat.

ANDREA: Yeh, tings really movin' good wid 'im, yuh nuh? But true mi neva know Taranto 'ad islands!

NIESHA: Fird time you come here an' you never heard dere have islands?

ANDREA: Fi dem islands cyan' be nuttin' like fi we islands— dem cya' be cramp up, cramp up like Fanon or Cavivia. Dem prob'ly spacious! Mi wa' tinkin tuh get a floral dress; sometin flowy fi ketch da island breeze. Mi tink sey mi need a badein' suit tuh go underneath it! Ohh mi know mi 'ad fi get a gold bikini! My-kal Kors (Michael Kors).

NIESHA: You does wase too much money.

ANDREA: I'm a lady, A' mus' fi look good!

NIESHA: You alone dat have to look good den?

ANDREA: Mi nah know wha' you're doin'. Mi already tell yuh sey some lipstick an' some nail palish would do you good every once in a while.

NIESHA: Me? I don' wasein' my money on ga'bage so.

ANDREA: E' nah cos' nuttin' at all. Mi get mi lipstick a' Dollarama; Wet an' Wile! Same place mi get mi Sally 'ansen nail palish. Dollarama 'ave, comb, sanitary napkin, lipsticks, Q-Tips, 'and (hand) weight, everyting unda da sun. A' wha dey nah sell, flea market 'ave it.

NIESHA: Dere we stay all day; morning, noon an' night.

ANDREA: Dollarama right across da street, go on your break.

NIESHA: After I finish stan' all day, you fink iz walk I want to walk across de strit on my break? Mwen (me) den?

NIESHA exits through the back with a bag full of garbage.

ANDREA: Yuh 'ave too much excuse. If yuh wan' look gud, nuttin' can stop yuh—

Enter ELDRICK.

Yuh deh early.

ELDRICK: As far as I know, I can come by any time I want.

ANDREA: Buh yuh neva. Yuh always a' pass jus' before we lack; jus' as I am leavin' out.

ELDRICK: You always does leave early.

ANDREA: Niesha always leave late.

ELDRICK: She back dere?

ANDREA: She might be.

ELDRICK: Tell her I dere.

ANDREA: She can 'ear you. She just nah respon'. Niesha?

NIESHA: Yeh!?

ELDRICK: Niesha!

NIESHA: **

ANDREA: See? She nah business wid yuh.

ELDRICK: I don' have too much time. Tell her iz me, nuh?

ANDREA: Of all a da girls who work in all da shop, why yuh fi choose 'er? Hm?

ELDRICK: What kind of question is dat?

ANDREA: Mi know sey many of us are available an' h'any girl would die fi a catch like yuh.

ELDRICK: Includin' you?

ANDREA: Mi already 'ave mi man, but if mi was single—

NIESHA comes back in from the back door.

NIESHA: *(To ANDREA.)* What?

ANDREA: Ur man.

ELDRICK: Hey.

NIESHA: Seem I cannot get a day in de week where I don' fine myself lookin' at you.

ELDRICK: Dat's a bad fing, princess?

NIESHA: I am busy woukin' (working).

ELDRICK: I am a hungry customer.

NIESHA: Ani can help you.

ANDREA: He don' want nuttin' mi 'ave.

ELDRICK: Am not here for food.

ANDREA: Yuh see?

NIESHA: Den what you come dere fuh? Wha' you come fuh?

ANDREA: Niesha, don' be foolish!

ELDRICK: I was doin' a job up de street; fought I would stop by.

NIESHA: What job?

ELDRICK: A construction site.

NIESHA: What site? Where it?

ELDRICK: Umm… you know if you go up de street an' turn round where you see—

NIESHA: Wha' you relly come for?

ELDRICK: **

ANDREA: **

NIESHA: **

ELDRICK: Alright. Dere goin an' have a comedy show playin' at a community centre by me next Fursday. I happen to get two ticket.

NIESHA: **

ELDRICK: I want to brin' you / wif me.

ANDREA: / Oh, She 'ould like dat.

NIESHA: No fanks.

ELDRICK: Why not?

NIESHA: I a'ready have plans.

ANDREA: Girl, dat's a lie.

NIESHA: I don' like comedy.

ANDREA: Dat's a likkle more closer tuh troot.

ELDRICK: You have a problem wif laughta?

ANDREA: She 'aven't got no sense of 'umour—

NIESHA: I just don' fine many fings funny. Most comedy show dey just talk a pile a nonsense. I fine I just laugh becaw iz sorry I sorry for de person.

ELDRICK: Which comedy shows have you been to?

ANDREA: She ain't been tuh none.

NIESHA: I been to a couple.

ANDREA: Where?

NIESHA: Girl! — In Fanon.

ANDREA: Where yuh deh from? Yuh see? Nobody funny nah live dere.

ELDRICK: It's different dere. Come with me. If you don' like it, we'll leave and do somefing else. I will bring you by de lake or somefing.

ANDREA: Da lake!

NIESHA: I don' like lakes.

ELDRICK: Okay not de lake—a park, or a garden.

ANDREA: Hmm Hmm!

NIESHA: I don'—

ELDRICK You don' like parks. It doesn' matter, da' is not de point— I just want to take you out. If I just keep seein' you at der restaurant when you're busy I'll never get to know you better. If you don' like it, we don' have to do it again.

NIESHA: You promise?

ANDREA: Why yuh stay suh mean?

ELDRICK: I mean I will still come by de restaurant.

NIESHA: For wha'?

ELDRICK: I like de chicken.

NIESHA: Dere have eleven odder Caribbean restaurant on dis same strit.

ANDREA: Yeh but fi we chicken da bes'.

ELDRICK: Exack'ly.

NIESHA: Well, I am not / interested.

ANDREA: Wha time e' da show deh Tursday?

ELDRICK: Nine p.m.

ANDREA: We'll lack up early. Pick 'er up a eight farty-five.

NIESHA: Excuse—

ELDRICK: Great!

ANDREA: *(To NIESHA.)* We nah really lack h'early. Mi can stay an' lack up, h'okay?

(To ELDRICK.) Dress code?

NIESHA: You mus' be goin', 'cause I never say—

ELDRICK: Somefing nice for an evenin' out.

ANDREA: Mi mek sure she brin' a change a clodes.

NIESHA: How you gon' do dat?

ANDREA: Watch me.

ELDRICK: Great. See you in a week and a likkle bit.

NIESHA: Papamet! (My god!)

ANDREA: We a see yuh before dat. You'll drop by in between.

ELDRICK: I might…Okay, I definitely will. What time again?

NIESHA walks to the back; kissing her teeth.

ANDREA: Eight-tirty.

NIESHA comes back.

NIESHA: Las' I check, dere closing at nine o clock!

ANDREA: Exactly.

NIESHA: I am not leavin' dis store before nine, so anyone who try to come for me even if iz one minute before will have to sit down dere an' wait!

ELDRICK: Okay. See you at nine, den.

NIESHA: Ya. You come an' see if I go anywhere wif you. I busy! I have fings to do!

ANDREA: *(To ELDRICK.)* Tek a piece a chickeen.

ELDRICK: Am not hungry.

ANDREA: Yes, yuh are; mi nah charge yuh nuttin.

NIESHA: You don' have no right to give away de chicken for free.

ANDREA: We 'aven't 'ad a customer in at least farty-five minute.

NIESHA: So how we goin' an account for de missin' food?

ANDREA Yuh tink sey h'Yvonne feh come 'round count out da food an' notice one piece of chickeen gone? Pass me a plastic.

NIESHA passes her a plastic bag.

NIESHA: You bein' defiant for defiance sake!

ANDREA: If she notice da piece chickeen gone, tell her mi eat it.

ELDRICK: I can pay for de food if you want.

NIESHA: Ye—

ANDREA: Nah, man; you 'ave a nice day, Eldricks!

ELDRICK: You too, Andrea.

NIESHA: *(To ANDREA.)* Ani, you take it too fa'.

ANDREA: Ani.

ELDRICK: Ani.

Niesha.

NIESHA: Ya, bye.

Exit ELDRICK.

Keep giving away de food to every one of your stupid boyfriends dat come by an' see how one of dese days you'll get us both in some kind of trouble.

ANDREA: Which stch'upid bwoyfrien'? Mi 'memba sey mi 'ave one.

NIESHA: Any of dem!

ANDREA: Far as I can r'memba dat one fi you bwoyfrien', 'im nah fi me.

NIESHA: I am not de one feedin' him for free!

ANDREA: So 'ee is your bwoyfrien', yuh jus' nah feed 'im?

NIESHA: A-las Ani! —

ANDREA: Yuh mus' try fi cool aff.

NIESHA: Yvonne is takin' a huge risk havin' us work dere—

ANDREA: Please, I been 'ere long enough to know 'ow dis 'ere work betta for 'er. Why yuh tink sey Donnie an' Susan work five-hour shifs an' we work nine or-or even sometimes eleven? Minimum wage is thirteen twenty-five an' seein 'ow long dem a work 'ere, dem prob'ly up tuh fifteen dollar a' hour. Meanwhile, we meking ten dollars a' hour. Eleven-hour shifs. Yuh can h'imagine sey da type of savings Yvonne save by hiring us under da table? Hm?

NIESHA: Se pa biznis mwen (not my business).

ANDREA: Tousands! Maybe 'undreds a tousands!

NIESHA: Da' nah de point!

ANDREA: E' is da point! A ooo it benefit?

NIESHA: How much you was makin' back home? What I was makin' as a home help was jus' as much work an' I was takin' home about a quarta of what I makin' dere now. Now, I collec'in my five hundred dollars at the end of ich (each) week. I sen' one hundred for my kids, put one hundred aside for my rent at de end of de monf, one hundred for my grocery, bus fare an' every penny of de res' I save it. Abby is fourteen an' Samuel is twelve, I have school fee, college, an' wif how smart dey are, university a few years afta dat; life is expensive.

Whatever Yvonne get from hiring us, I don' key'ah (care). I get to put my life togeder an' put somefing aside for my chil'ren too. Dat's what dat matta to me, eh. An' only way I get it, is from she helpin' me to try an' make a life in dis country. She good to me an' I don' want to cheat her; simple. She keep her mouth shut. Now what if she realize I dere closin' up her shop early an' giving away food for free?

ANDREA: Mi nah eat food today if dat mek yuh feel better.

NIESHA: Not dat I saying.

ANDREA: Yeh, it is. Mi give da food guh 'way suh mi nah tek no more so when Yvonne come a count up da food—which she nah guh do—she nah guh ketch wise.

NIESHA: **

ANDREA: **

NIESHA: I'll give you some from mines.

ANDREA: Yuh' too careful, Niesha. Yuh need fi tek more risk. Dat young man clearly like you.

NIESHA: He haven' got nuffin to do wiv dis.

ANDREA: 'Im 'ave everyting tuh do wit everyting!

NIESHA: I come dere to try an' make a way for my family.

ANDREA: An' dere's more dan one way tuh look 'bout it.

NIESHA: I not like you, eh. I haven' had good chance wif men.

ANDREA: Ooo 'as? Tell me sey, which ooman in a 'ole a di world 'ad good chances wit men?

NIESHA: I don' trust dem.

ANDREA: Yuh don' need fi trus 'im all da way, suh. Yuh nah need sey fi tell out your 'art (heart) an' soul an' everyting. All yuh a need is someone yuh can trust enough to do you a favour.

NIESHA: Sh!

ANDREA: An' a 'ee look like da type ooo might be willin'.

NIESHA: Lowa your voice, nuh?

ANDREA: Yuh jus 'ave fi work on 'im.

NIESHA: I tell you to low down your voice!

ANDREA: Yuh 'ave a' opportunity; yuh bes' tek it. Mi sey loud an' clear; TEK IT!

Yuh nah h'even look for it; 'im jus fall right in your lap! Right when yuh was dere a work lookin da way you normally look.

When yuh go out wit dat man yuh bes' mek a' effort. Yuh 'ave nice dress; put one on. Wear a nice padded bra, show a likkle lace, put powder on a your face, comb your hair, put some lipstick.

NIESHA: I never leave de house wifout combin' my hair.

ANDREA: You still 'ave a few mont, go out wit 'im every now an' den, mek 'im feel nice, if 'im want it, nah put up too much a fight. Yuh nah mek it too easy or seem like yuh want it too bad, but also nah put up too much a fight. Play it cool, see 'ow much 'im into you an' den, when da time is right, mek your move.

NIESHA: I just mit (meet) de fella, Andrea.

ANDREA: Work on 'im. Nah tek too lang. Yuh 'ave fi see if 'im a 'elp yuh.

NIESHA: You min tell him?

ANDREA: If 'im trus'wordy (trustworthy).

NIESHA: You don' min (mean) for me to tell him?

ANDREA: Yuh nah mus fi come right out an spill da beans. You could suggest.

NIESHA: Suggest what? Dat too risky— you tell Malcolm?

ANDREA: Dat not da point.

NIESHA: Have you?!

Andrea, iz dangerous! You don' know who he is! What if he—

ANDREA: Mi know sey a ooo 'ee is; 'im a good man an' 'im cares about me.

NIESHA: Yes, but you don' know who he might tell.

ANDREA: Mi nah tell yuh sey mi wan fi tell him; Mi jus' sey mi might do it.

NIESHA: I hope you know what you' doin'—

ANDREA: Mi nah decide yet.

NIESHA: —de more people you tell, de more chances somefing could go wrong.

ANDREA: Look! A dis fi mi game. Mi mek it up as mi guh 'long an' mi figure out ow mi tink sey it a go.

NIESHA: Well, I have a game too an' if you don' want me in yours, you should stop interferin' in mines.

ANDREA: You 'ave a game? You? Seem tuh me like you wasn' playin' at all.

NIESHA: Of course I have a game. I am not dere on holiday. If I fine someone to help me out, you can bet dat I will take it— But it have to be for de right reason. Dere have to be some kine of true affection an' I am not goin' an degrade myself to get it.

ANDREA: So, what a mi a do is degrade myself?

NIESHA: It came from your mouf, not mines.

ANDREA: Bes yuh watch how yuh talk to me, mi nat nah ratid fool!

NIESHA: Noffin' I say'd was specifically referring to you.

ANDREA: Yuh tink sey you so 'i (high) up an' me nah have nuh pride. Yuh nah tink sey Malcolm love me.

NIESHA: You have your mefods (methods), I have mines.

ANDREA: Malcolm a good man an' what 'im an' me deh pan is good. 'im tek me everywhere mi need tuh guh, 'im 'ave a gud jahb, 'im pleasant, 'im nah abuse me. As far as I can see fi me game guh lang (is going along) betta dan yours. An' fi mi pickney guh reap da benefit far sooner dan yours eva will becaw fi dem mammy wah willing tuh mek whateva sacrifice she 'ad tuh fi mek sure dem 'ave da bes' life dem possibly can 'ave. Mek yuh stay dere a turn down dates wit perfectly decent men dat jus' a fall into your lap an' see where it a tek yuh.

Wha' yuh wan? A knight in shinin' armour? A 'orse (horse)? Stay dere an' wait while mi tek advantage of my man ooo is perfectly acceptable. Wait an' see your chil'ren dem a struggle fi get fru while fi me soar up to da stars—

NIESHA: Koute sa (listen to that); stay out of my business. Not to fix me up wif no date wif no man again. I don' need no mouf'piss (mouthpiece) to talk for me.

Long, uncomfortable beat. NIESHA pulls a garbage bin into the open, presses the garbage down and ties the bag shut.

An' stop leevin' de ga'bage in dere until it pile up pile up sky high—it stinkin'! Next fing you know we' gonna have rats!

ANDREA: One a'ready a run 'round behin' me.

NIESHA drops the garbage bag back in the bin. The phone rings.

Customer.

ANDREA answers it.

Good afternoon. What can I get fur you today?

NIESHA finishes with the garbage.

Yeh, we still have dat. Come 'roun in ten… yeh.

She hangs up.

NIESHA: I not goin' an' be a foolish. What I have to do to make him like me?

ANDREA: 'Im already do. Nah fi tek dis nuh way, but mi always di tink sey you 'ad a nice shape backside. Yuh ken even see it unda your uniform. Imagine 'ow nice it a look in a fitted, ledda skirt. Mi just tell yuh sey.

Exit ANDREA with the garbage. NIESHA lingers, sees a reflection of her butt, she smiles a little, then goes back to her work.

Scene 4

ANDREA and MALCOLM make out in the back of his RAV4. She's not as into it as she usually is. He notices, she shrugs it off and tries to get back into it.

MALCOLM: Ani?

ANDREA: Mmm?

MALCOLM: I love you.

ANDREA stops.

ANDREA: Love me wha? Yuh nah love me.

MALCOLM: Yes, I do. How you gonna tell me how I feel?

ANDREA: B'caw— wah' sey yuh love 'bout me?

MALCOLM: Everyting.

ANDREA: Wha' everyting?

MALCOLM: Your pretty-pretty eyes.

ANDREA: Mm hmm.

MALCOLM: Your sexy body.

ANDREA: Mmm hmm.

MALCOLM: The way all man stare at you when you dance in the party—

ANDREA: Man, yuh lef' da Caribbean from small buh da Caribbean man nah fi lef yuh.

She grabs his face and they kiss.

Shift. NIESHA and ELDRICK sitting on a park bench.

ELDRICK: I knew you would like it.

NIESHA: E' was okay.

ELDRICK: I heard you laughing!

NIESHA: De secon' fella was nice. I like de joke he make about Black people chuch.

ELDRICK: How dey should be de new diet because you reachin' church at nine A.M., dey have you jumpin', screamin' and runnin' about de place all day and den you don' get home to eat until afta free!

NIESHA: People does pass out in chuch, wi! An' you fink iz spirit dat enta dem. But relly, iz just food dat haven' enta dem!

ELDRICK: *(Laughing.)* You see?!

NIESHA: And chuch hot! You eva been in a chuch wif fans?

ELDRICK: Dat work? Nah—

NIESHA: Ya, I did take a joke in dat, but de res' of his ack (act) was dry—

ELDRICK: You lyin'!

NIESHA: Real!

ELDRICK: He have annoda show in a couple weeks; I can pick you up afta work one time.

Beat.

NIESHA: Yeah.

ELDRICK: Yeah? Dat's cool.

NIESHA: Yes. Yes.

ELDRICK: Cool, cool. I will arrange it den.

You look great in dat dress.

NIESHA: Yes, but it scratchin'.

ELDRICK: I could help wif dat if you like...

NIESHA: ***

ELDRICK: The night is still young. Wanna go to a park or somefing?

NIESHA: No.

ELDRICK: A late night movie?

NIESHA: No fanks.

ELDRICK: Okay. A—

NIESHA: You can take me home.

ELDRICK: Okay—

NIESHA: My home.

ELDRICK: Dat's fine Niesha. Am not tryin' to force you to lime wif me. De date is over, de date is over.

I assume you live in Scarborough.

NIESHA: Finch an' Sewells.

Shift. MALCOLM and ANDREA in the car.

MALCOLM: I do love you, dough.

ANDREA: Yuh nah fi sey tings yuh nah mean.

MALCOLM: I do. What I gotta lie for?

ANDREA: Love is not about sexy body an' pretty pretty eye.

MALCOLM: I know.

ANDREA: It' not about ooo fi watch ooo on da dance floor.

MALCOLM: I know all dat.

ANDREA: Yuh wan' tuh love me?

MALCOLM: If you want me to.

ANDREA: Becaw mi nah tink sey mi eva di' need love.

MALCOLM: You're an interestin' woman, Andrea. What do you want if you don't want love? Like? Would you prefer me to say I really really like you? I want you?

She puts his hand down her shirt.

ANDREA: Nah. Mi need fi know sey we have trus, like... Me a' you—'ave trus' ova anybody else.

MALCOLM: Okay, like...?

ANDREA: Yuh fi 'ave mi back an' ben' backward fi 'elp me out, yuh know? Dat mi need—a real man—a salid man!

MALCOLM: Wow.

ANDREA: Mi need someone ooo can 'elp mi out, yuh know?

MALCOLM: Like what? Money or something? Because I'm not really the kind a guy dat really gives girls money.

ANDREA: Nat money—

MALCOLM: Like I always pay when we go out, but—

He takes his hand out of her shirt.

ANDREA: I have my own money, stchu'pid!

MALCOLM: Yow, dis kinda a vibez kill, dough.

ANDREA: 'Ow yuh mean?

MALCOLM: — like we were having a vibez, still, and you just got deep, like… man.

ANDREA: We were jus' 'avin' a conversyation. You start wit da love ting and I was just tryin'—

MALCOLM: I was just tryna make you feel nice so we could chill, you know?

ANDREA: Like… ya, I know.

MALCOLM: Just a relax ting.

ANDREA: Mmhm.

MALCOLM: So, you good or you feelin' different?

ANDREA: I'm good.

MALCOLM: Ya?

ANDREA: Ya.

MALCOLM: For real?

ANDREA: I'm awesome!

MALCOLM: I know you are.

Back in control, she straddles him.

NIESHA and ELDRICK walk toward her home.

NIESHA: You lef' de vee'cle runnin'.

ELDRICK: Far as I understan', Iz not stay I stayin' dere too long.

NIESHA: You shouldn't trust dat strit dere.

ELDRICK: My old car is nofing anybody want to steal. And if dey try, I'll be happy to Bruce Lee on dem.

NIESHA: *(Pointing to a house.)* Iz right ova dere.

ELDRICK: I'll walk you to de door. Dis is a nice place. Iz yours?

NIESHA: Basement.

ELDRICK: Nice. You been dere a while? It comfortable?

NIESHA: It suit me.

ELDRICK: Noffing like having a place to call home.

Beat. They walk to the basement door.

I had a nice time wif you, Niesha.

NIESHA: Yeah. Me too.

ELDRICK: I like you.

They kiss. They kiss a lot. They kiss 'til she's pressed up against the door. NIESHA backs away; pushing ELDRICK off her.

ELDRICK: I will call you.

NIESHA: You don' have my number.

ELDRICK: Neva did stop me before.

ELDRICK walks back toward his car. NIESHA watches him leave.

Scene 5

Jerk Pork Castle, the next day, minutes to close. ANDREA is on the phone with a customer.

ANDREA: Yuh see, mi di tell yuh it wa' fourteen twenty-five, buh we did nah 'ave no change suh mi axe yuh "do you wan' fi mek a donation?" An' yuh did, I r'memba… 'Ow you mean tuh wha'? Tuh—

She finds a cardboard donation box with some Black kids on it.

The Christian Children's Orphanage School Fund. Tanks. Ya, come back nex week, yuh 'ear (you hear)?

Door chimes. The women start their shop closing procedures.

(To NIESHA.) It a busy d'yay today!

NIESHA: Yep. Busiest one in a few wiks!

ANDREA: An' mi tank god for dat. Yuh deh look pan da new schedule?

NIESHA: Briefly.

ANDREA: h'Yvonne cut back a mi howers (hours)! Yours get cut tuh?

NIESHA: Nope.

ANDREA: Yuh lucky. She neva di like me.

NIESHA: She like everybody.

ANDREA: Ya, ya h'Yvonne biggest fan.

Beat.

Yuh still nah tell me 'ow yur date guh.

NIESHA: Hmm?

ANDREA: Was it gud?

NIESHA: It was okay.

ANDREA: Yuh fi get… a little bit?

NIESHA: Inappropriate.

ANDREA: Mi tink sey yuh neva; yuh been miserable an' uptight all day. Be 'appy (happy)! If business stay like dis, mi get mi hours back an' you fi get more shifts wit me!

Beat.

Yuh tink sey da restaurant fi close down?

NIESHA: I don' know, nuh.

ANDREA: Where yuh fi go if it do?

NIESHA: I cannot fink about such fings.

ANDREA: Dat's me; always finkin… Mi know someone who do office cleaning at night. E' nah pay as well, dough.

NIESHA: Does not pay at all.

ANDREA: 'ow you know dat?

NIESHA: —listen, you self just say business pickin' up, so stop bein' so negative! Me alone wipe down all de tables an' me alone go' put up all de chair. Den, you gonna traipse outta here early, as usual and wonder why your hours get cut!

ANDREA: I been tryin' tuh figure out why yuh so wretched all da time an mi tink sey mi fin'lly put mi finger pan it.

NIESHA: ***

ANDREA: When a da las' time you been wit a man?

NIESHA: ***

ANDREA: You prob'ly 'aven't 'ad a man touch yuh since sey yuh make ur son ten… eleven years ago? Dat not 'ealthy. Gyal need fi...release—too much a stress.

NIESHA: Yes, iz relly stressful, for true.

ANDREA: Release!

She laughs.

NIESHA: Sammy did not rich (reach) home last night; my boy. Abigail call me in a panic dis early mornin', before she go school.

ANDREA: She don' know where 'im stay?

NIESHA: He rich home, early in de morning. She say he was smellin' like alcohol or drugs, or…

ANDREA: Mi 'ope (hope) sey she give 'im one lick inna 'im 'ide (hide). Sometime dat all dey need—

NIESHA: Try she try to call me las' night while I was out havin' good time wif Eldricks.

ANDREA: Yuh nah 'ear ur phone?

NIESHA: I don't have no data and I couldn' connec' to wifi 'til I rich home.

And when I rich home I was feelin' nice from my stoopid date. I shower, an'—I forget all about checkin' my children! Am a bad modda! An now look at de trouble!

ANDREA: Yuh nah bod. De children dem wort'less! Dey know sey dere mammy guh foreign fi try mek some movements fi 'elp dem; why dey nah fi behave dem likkle selves?!

NIESHA: I always check my phone before I close my eyes—

ANDREA: An' if you know las' night, wha' yuh a guh do? Yuh guh wrangle up ur bwoy through ur phone?

NIESHA: I would had call people I know—my village! Somebody—

ANDREA: Ahhh, dat nah work.

NIESHA: I have people lookin' out for me—

ANDREA: Does nat matta! I tell yuh—Me neva tell yuh about mi bwoy 'Arvey?

NIESHA: No, only Benny—Benjamin.

ANDREA: 'Arvey i' mi oldest. Den Benjamin, Alicia, an' LeAnne. Mi jus' turn fifteen when mi 'ave 'im. Mi nah get fi finish school so mi guh work in da city wit mi sista. Mi did all kine a job; affice cleanin', nursin' 'ome, waitressin', 'air dressin', sellin' slippers pan da roadside— sometime all at once— just so mi children neva di 'ave fi feel like dem wah missin' nuttin'.

Bwoy, sometimes mi nah know sey 'ow I mi do it—buh dem always 'ad food pon da tyable, clean uniform an' shoe.

By about fourteen, fifteen, 'Arvey start brin'in fings inna da 'ouse, clodes, shoes, cellphones, dat mi know mi neva di buy an' tell me "a fren gi'e it tuh 'im." Which fren?!

Well, mi fine out which frens an' wha kine a activity dey was doin an' mi drag out mi son out a dere house by 'im ear.

'Im was cryin' sayin' I embarrass 'im.

Mi axe 'im wha' 'im wan'? Wha 'im really wan'? Becaw if dere is someting 'im need an' I can'na provide, mi work 'til mi lose two a mi finger—tuh get it far 'im.

Beat.

'Im stay 'ome a few days, yeh… buh den 'im jus' guh back behin' 'im frens.

Days mi nah see 'im—couldna track 'im downk. Next fing, all inna da news; some rough bwoys guh an' rob up foreign couple a gun-pa'int. Ran-sack dem 'ouse an' lef dem bleed up, bleed up.

Next call mi get from 'im wah colleck.

NIESHA: Where he be now?

ANDREA: 'Im still still dere a prison.

NIESHA: An' what you goin' an do?

ANDREA: What I guh do? What I guh do?!

NIESHA: I mus' get Sammy out… my boy is smart!

ANDREA: An' my boy?

NIESHA: My girl— I see dem makin' eyes at her when she walk down de strits, and I fink she likes it—maybe… Grown men! Old enough to be my fada—

ANDREA: Nuffin' new. Same fing a gwan a Caviva.

NIESHA: —because dey have fings dat likkle girls want—lunch money, cell phones—

ANDREA: Attention dem a tink dem a only get once.

Beat.

Tell har de attention stop as de belly grows.

NIESHA: I gotta see how I can make fings move quicker—

ANDREA: Now yuh finking. Fink. Like. Me.

NIESHA: I'll do anyfing. Eldrick, Celdrick, whoever!

ANDREA: Now yuh a talk.

NIESHA: Groom me! Teach me your ways!

Fucking awkward.

You gettin' any closer wiv Malcolm?

ANDREA: *(She shrugs.)* Mmm.

NIESHA: Wha'd you do last night?

ANDREA: Wha' yuh tink?

NIESHA: Nofin' else?

ANDREA: ***

NIESHA: You did tell him?

ANDREA: We 'ad fun, mi guh 'ome, work da dyay, dat's it.

NIESHA: If you was to tell him, you fink, he would help?

ANDREA: I don' know.

NIESHA: Tell him den! Try! But be careful! But again, you cannot be so careful you miss your chance to try. I keep tellin you "be careful, be careful," but—do what you have to do; save your child! Don't listen to me.

ANDREA: Trus me, mi neva was tekkin' mi cues from you. Mi axe 'im fi pick me up again tuh'night; mi a sweet 'im up like 'im neva been sweet up before. An' if sey tuhnight, mi nah get wha' mi need from 'im mi jus' move right along.

NIESHA: Dat's right.

ANDREA: Mi nah fi degrade mi'self. Mi cy'anna keep waiting wid 'im an' a miss my shot.

NIESHA: Right! Right!

ANDREA: Mi nah fi beg 'im legal pyapa; mi nah fi beg nuh man nuttin! 'E cy'an gimmie wha' mi need, mi know sey mi can fine someone in dis damn place ooo can.

Beat.

NIESHA: Dere mus' be annoda option from dat.

ANDREA: What kine a option, Niesha? Mi already tell yuh, mi nah guh back a Caviva; nah! Malcolm e nat da only man deh pan all a' Scarborough, pan all a' Canada! Malcolm would be a fool tuh nah keep me! Mi wuh give 'im everyting.

Car lights shine on their faces. A Toyota RAV4.

NIESHA: Go ahead.

ANDREA: Nah man, mi 'elp you lack up.

NIESHA: I will lock up de back.

ANDREA opens the front door. MALCOLM enters.

MALCOLM: Hey.

ANDREA: By'aby.

He kisses her.

MALCOLM: You ready to go?

She nods.

Niesha, you good.

NIESHA: Yes, am excellent.

MALCOLM: You need a ride home?

NIESHA: Bus.

MALCOLM: You sure?

NIESHA: Yep. Bus.

They lock up the front and exit the restaurant.

ANDREA: Bye, Niesha. Nah fi worry yuhself; yur boy will sart 'imself out.

Beat.

NIESHA: Tomorrow.

ANDREA: Yeh.

Exit NIESHA.

ANDREA and MALCOLM in the car.

MALCOLM: You gonna change?

ANDREA: Nat sure yet.

MALCOLM: Where 're you feeling to go?

ANDREA: Mi nah really mek plan.

MALCOLM: Okay, well, we could grab a drink at the sports bar down the street—

ANDREA: Mi nah really wan' fi go no' weh. Mi jus' wan fi pull up, yeh, right 'ere, yeh.

MALCOLM: In the parking lot?

ANDREA: Yeh.

MALCOLM: Okay.

Long beat.

We could—

ANDREA: Nah, mi nah—

MALCOLM: So, you want me to take you home or—

ANDREA: Las' night mi da try fi tell yuh sump'um but, as usual, tings got 'eated an' mi nah get a chance fi say wha' mi 'ad tuh.

MALCOLM: Alright.

ANDREA: Actually, you wasn' interested. Suh mi cuh see, wha' mi wuh tinkin' jus' would'nah mek sense. Nat wit you.

MALCOLM: I'm not understanding.

ANDREA: Mi nah tink sey tings a guh work out between us. Sarry.

MALCOLM: Why?

ANDREA: Mi wan' sump'um mi nah langa tink yuh can gi'me. A commitment. A salid man.

MALCOLM: You're right. That's something I certainly can't give you.

ANDREA: Why nat?

MALCOLM: Because I can't. Dat's it.

ANDREA: Well, dat I need.

MALCOLM: But you know I'm not interested in dat. You always knew.

ANDREA: How I know when yuh neva di tell me?

MALCOLM: Yeh, I did. I told you, we're just having fun. I axed you—a few times, I remember—if that was okay with you, that we just have fun.

ANDREA: Yeh, but when mi axe yuh sey fi guh on a real dyate, yuh tek me, more dan once.

MALCOLM: Because it was fun; dat's what I like. And I like you—Andrea. You are like the queen of fun. But a relationship...nah. I'm sorry—

ANDREA: Yuh know wha'? Nah worry yuhself 'bout it.

MALCOLM: That's what you called me here to say?

Beat.

I wouldn't make a good boyfriend to you anyway. I had one girlfriend in, like, my whole life and you can axe her... it wasn't good.

ANDREA: Mi cyan't wase nuh more time wit you, Malcolm. Mi 'ave stuff tuh sart (sort) out.

MALCOLM: Can I give you a ride home?

Beat.

Don't be like Niesha.

ANDREA: No, mi tek da ride. Mi tink sey mi a get blister from dese stch'upid shoe. Walmart still open? Drap (drop) mi dere mek mi buy a new one.

Scene 6

A few weeks later. NIESHA and ELDRICK walk through a park, talking and holding hands. NIESHA laughs at something ELDRICK says, he puts his arm around her. They stop walking; share a long kiss.

NIESHA: You been stoppin' by de rest'rant a lot de pass few wiks. Like I see you every ordder (other) day!

ELDRICK: Ya, sometimes am not even out; am just at home and I dere wonderin, what is Niesha doin', nuh? How she done her hair? Can I put a smile on her sweet likkle lips?

Especially since I seen more an' more you workin' alone now dat Yvonne cut back so many hours from Ani.

NIESHA: Since Island Vibes open across de strit, business been rel slow. Yvonne had to recuperate somehow.

ELDRICK: Fast food chains really is de devil.

NIESHA: Especially de ones dat preten to be aufentic Caribbean cuisine.

ELDRICK: Dey does start out aufentic.

NIESHA: Sure! Until de white people discova dem an' dey start usin' a likkle less pepper in de sauce.

ELDRICK: Hey, say what you want, but white people does bring dere money.

NIESHA: But dey don' have no tase—

ELDRICK: Matters not. You can have all der taste in der world, but if you have no money…

NIESHA: Persons dat know rel good food still come by us, but dose fly-by-night customers get attrak by pretty sign, bright light an' crowd.

Beat.

I glad you does come, don', for true. It does get lonesome workin' dere alone.

ELDRICK: So, I mus' come by more often?

NIESHA: You does come by enough.

ELDRICK: Every day? Twice a day?

NIESHA: No, please, you will make me to don' sell no food.

He kisses her neck.

ELDRICK: Well, sell me somefing else, nah?

NIESHA: No. I said no.

He kisses her a lot.

I had a nice time, Eldricks.

ELDRICK: Me too.

NIESHA: I don' fink I never seen such a nice park!

ELDRICK: I was surprise when you did say you had not been dere before.

NIESHA: De cinema was nice too. We can check anodda film nex wik?

ELDRICK: Of course. I would love dat.

Beat.

Now, am gonna share somefing wif you. My name is Eldrick Mathieu Phillips. Next week I will be thirty years of age—

NIESHA: A baby.

ELDRICK: I know.

Beat.

I 'ave been leavin' (living) in Canada for… nearly ten years now? Ya. I have one kid; a son—twelve. His back home wif his modder. His into music. I did try and send for him but he not yet ready. He too attach to his modder. But whenever he ready, ou know? Now, your turn.

NIESHA: For what?

ELDRICK: To tell me a likkle more about you.

NIESHA: Why?

ELDRICK: I just did.

NIESHA: I did not axe you.

ELDRICK: We been datin' a few weeks now and I feel I do not know noffing about you. What is your full name? Do you have any hobbies? Do you have any kids? How long have you been here? How long you plan to stay?

NIESHA: What kine of question is dat?

ELDRICK: Which one?

NIESHA: Don' play sot sot (stupid) wif me; de las' one.

ELDRICK: Valid question.

NIESHA: No! Insult you want to insult me?

ELDRICK: How?

NIESHA: Okay, I gone an' tell you sumfing; I did not axe you to see me an' I for shore did not axe you anyfing about yourself. Wif me, what you see is what you get, so jus' see me, like me an' forget about de res'. If you don' like dese conditions, you more dan welcome to go about your business.

ELDRICK: Really? Niesha, you know you can trus' me, right? Am just trying to get a better sense of de woman am fallin' in love wif.

NIESHA: All you fellas so love to use dat word, love, when most of you don' even takin' de sense in it.

ELDRICK: Why you fink you know so much about what I know?

NIESHA: I know dat I never met a fella who did know de true sense of de word love an' I have two chirren at home to prove it.

ELDRICK: Well, I mean it!

NIESHA: I can'na believe—

ELDRICK: Tell me about yourself, Niesha. De more you get to know me you will know that I am a man of my wuds (words).

Beat.

I will proteck you and take care of you as long as you are honest wif me.

NIESHA: Wha' you mean "proteck an take care of me"?

ELDRICK: I mean whatever you need me to mean.

NIESHA: I'm smarter dan you fink.

ELDRICK: So am I.

He kisses her. She's into it.

NIESHA: My fick accent will tell you iz not too long I been living dere in Canada.

ELDRICK: How long is not too long?

NIESHA: Less dan you.

ELDRICK: Less dan a year?

NIESHA: Guess you could say dat.

ELDRICK: Less dan six months?

Beat.

Baby?

NIESHA: Iz possible.

Beat.

ELDRICK: You have two chir'ren?

NIESHA: A boy an' a girl.

ELDRICK: You does allow your boyfriends to meet dem?

NIESHA: Did I tell you I have boyfrens?

ELDRICK: Are dey here? Your kids?

NIESHA: No. Dey stay back home.

ELDRICK: Wif dere fadder?

NIESHA: Too many questions—

ELDRICK: You would like dem here wif you?

NIESHA: Eldricks, who doesn' want dey chil'ren in dey foot twenty-four seven?

Beat.

ELDRICK: And you work for Yvonne, under der table, cash, long hours, untraced...

NIESHA: Eldricks, I'm ready to—

ELDRICK: How much time you have lef?

NIESHA: For wha'?

ELDRICK: To stay in de country?

NIESHA: Who tell you is leave I leaving?

ELDRICK: I know you dere illegal. Iz quite regular; noffing to hide.

NIESHA: You can fink what you wan'; you don' have proof!

ELDRICK: I did tell you to be honest because you can trus' me.

NIESHA: Gade biznis ou (mind your business)!

ELDRICK: You did not get a work permit to come and work in a Caribbean restaurant in Scarborough for a few monf. No way—someone connect you wif Yvonne; she does it all de time.

NIESHA: Dis is why I hate you! All of you wif your love!

ELDRICK: I can help you. You know dat, right?

NIESHA: Move from me.

ELDRICK: I am not like de odders. You can trus' me.

NIESHA: You wanna drive me or I will walk to de bus stop?

Beat.

ELDRICK: You wanna stay here. You need your papers and de easiest way for you to get dem is frew me; I have my citizenship. Don't tell me you never fought about it.

Beat.

NIESHA: In government you workin' or what?

ELDRICK: Re'lly? I lookin' like I work for government? Driving a Corolla? I could never be hired by immigration; I came in de country illegal too.

NIESHA: You have your papers now?

ELDRICK: Nearly six years.

NIESHA: How you did get your status?

ELDRICK: I got set up. Dere are ways.

Beat.

NIESHA: I have fought about— fine'in a man to help me out.

ELDRICK: Good. So, am your man. Easy. Marry me, Niesha. You like me, am crazy about you and iz a perfect situation— Love. Wow! Dat's not what I had planned for my proposal but, dere it is.

NIESHA: Just like dat, you want to marry me?

ELDRICK: Yes.

NIESHA: Why?

ELDRICK: Because I love you… like I said.

NIESHA: Why else?

ELDRICK: Wha' you mean? Dat's de reason! I want to help you out. When I came, okay, I had to get a work and one of my partners let me use his S.I.N number for a while. Afta dat, he did help me fine a woman who was interested to marry me. We were not in love or noffing like dat, so once I got set up, we went our own ways and dere I am. Now I am willing to do the same for you; except, I love you and fink you will be a great real wife.

NIESHA: Why iz so easy for me? I neva get nuffing simple before an' now you just want to mek a wife out of me an' I don' have to do nuffing for you?

ELDRICK: I wouldn't say you don't have to do noffing. You are not going to sit 'round my apartment and not do noffing all day. Wha, did you expeck to lie on de couch and watch *Young and Restless*?

NIESHA: Of course not.

ELDRICK: I mean, I don't want dis to feel like an arrangement; I want you to be my real wife, undastan?

NIESHA: Like what?

ELDRICK: Like what wives do. Cook for me, keep da house clean, give me love like I give you.

NIESHA: Sex?

ELDRICK: Of course; what kind of marriage—

NIESHA: I understan'.

ELDRICK: Immigration's stricter now, dey will want evidence so we have to make fings look real. Understand?

NIESHA: Yes. All of dat is fine wif me.

ELDRICK: I'll start your papers as soon as we sign da marriage licence.

NIESHA: Okay. Sounds good.

ELDRICK: It's more dan good.

NIESHA: Relly. Iz relly great. Iz a great fing.

What about my chil'ren; you would let me sen' for dem?

ELDRICK: ... Eventually, yes. Of course, but dese fings does take time, you know dat.

NIESHA: I know. I have to get my permanent residence furse. But once we married, dat should not take long. An' it should not take long to get my kids because bof of dem are undda age, so...

ELDRICK: Exactly.

NIESHA: Dey would not want to kip (keep) such young kids apart from dere modder.

ELDRICK: As long as you keep workin' because I don' have money to support two chir'ren. I still have mine back home, so…

NIESHA: Of course! I complitely understan'. I would not expeck. I been woukin for my kids. I been savin' for dem since when I come! Dey can go school Canada. Get dere education an' job. Abby can get pat-time job soon. By de time she come she would be woukin' edge.

ELDRICK: It's okay, Niesha. I want you, so I want your kids too.

NIESHA: How soon ken it happen? If I was to say yes, when we could do it?

ELDRICK: It'd have to be pretty soon. I imagine you're supposed to go back soon.

NIESHA: Supposed to go back nex monf.

ELDRICK: So, we'll have to do it soon. Let us give owaselves two monfs?

NIESHA: Less woulda be better. Even a couple wiks would be fine.

ELDRICK: Okay, I'll book da earliest date I can get widdin a month. We'll work fas.

Okay— We'll have to keep it low key; do you care about da venue?

NIESHA: No.

ELDRICK: Dress? Guess list?

NIESHA: I don' care about nuffing.

ELDRICK: I'll look after it den. I'll look about all da specifics.

NIESHA: Okay. You shore you want to do dis?

ELDRICK: Are you sure you want to do dis?

NIESHA: Iz all I ever wanted. I would a fool to refuse.

ELDRICK: Yes, you would.

He kisses her.

NIESHA: Eldricks, ou say on bonne nom (you are a good man). I have been blessed, God!

He kisses her again.

De best man I eva meet.

ELDRICK: This is goin' to be great. Of course, I'll need a likkle bit of change to cover da wedding coss and da licence and everyfing. You know dat, right?

NIESHA: Yes. I imagine you would not go out of pocket for my sake.

ELDRICK: But I love you, and I'll spen' all my money on you in time.

NIESHA: I understan'.

ELDRICK: Good. You will have to pay de fees to file your papers.

NIESHA: Of course! I have some savings. How much you fink it will coss?

ELDRICK: Eeemm... lemme run it by some of my padnas. Dere have some fellas who will have a betta idea how much dese fing dere cossin'. Will work it out.

NIESHA: Okay. No problem.

ELDRICK: Not to worry yourself for now. We will talk about all of dat later. Give me a week or so to come back to you wif all de specifics. It can get complicated and—

NIESHA: Yes. Iz okay.

ELDRICK: I love you, dough.

NIESHA: Yes. Fank you. Yes. Yes! Mewci, Fank you. Fank you! But Eldricks, how comes?

ELDRICK: You yourself said iz God's work. He brought us togedder. Now you want to axe him why? Neva question de mos' high—

NIESHA: Of cou'se. Fanks (thanks), eh Eldricks!

They continue walking.

ELDRICK: Iz getting late now. I guess you're ready to go home? Let all of dis soak in?

NIESHA: Yes. An', you can stay— if you have noffing else doing.

ELDRICK: I— You sure?

NIESHA: Yeh. I have some meat season in de fridge dere. It's enough to share for two.

Scene 7

Jerk Pork Castle. The following week. New Skool Fanonian tune. ANDREA is postering the store with posters saying "PRE-CARNIVAL BLOCK-O. FRIDAY JULY 29TH. JERK PORK CASTLE BACK PARKING LOT. 9 TIL LATE. IT'S GONNA BE LIT!" A customer walks by.

ANDREA: Yes bassy! Nah forget a nex Friday we a 'ave pre-carnival block-o. Come 'round da back-parkin lat. It'a gwan tun up, mi tell yuh! Tell a yuh friens.

NIESHA enters, dancing to the song. She's wukking like she never wuk before. ANDREA dances with her.

ANDREA: Hmm! Yuh love dat song ee?

NIESHA: Love it!

ANDREA: Ar maybe yuh just 'appy!

NIESHA laughs.

Dat's da look of a bride to be! Mi 'appy far yuh man!

NIESHA: Fank YOU!

ANDREA: Yuh 'ave all a' wha' you need?

NIESHA: I fink so. I just must get somefing to put in my hair.

ANDREA: Veil?

NIESHA: I should wear veil?

ANDREA: Yeh, man!

NIESHA: I was only goin' an wear one of dem likkle fings dat does co'va de top of de foehead. Wha' dey call'in dem again? Birdcage? Blusher.

ANDREA: Yeh. Dem pretty too. Buh guh all out! Iz ur wedding! Do wha' yuh wan'!

NIESHA: Iz suppose to be low-key.

ANDREA: I don' know what dat means— We mus' fi get yuh a nice lingerie, yeh?

NIESHA: For what?

ANDREA: **

NIESHA: Not necessary.

ANDREA: Mi mus' tek yuh meet my guy inna da flea market. A dere mi buy all mi pretty lacey brazzier an' panty set—ten dolla or less. Come wid garta belt an' everyting!

NIESHA: Dat would be nice.

ANDREA: 'Course! Mi tek yuh a' Sunday. Don' mention it.

NIESHA: We mus' close de shop a likkle early tonight, dere.

ANDREA: Hold on—who dis?

NIESHA: Eldrick passin' by afta wouk and I want to mek sure I smellin' nice. Wipe some gris off my face.

ANDREA: Mi know jus wha yuh mean.

NIESHA: And I am shore you have some place to go too.

ANDREA: Nah.

NIESHA: What about dat new fella?

ANDREA: Nah.

NIESHA: Why?

ANDREA: Mi nah like 'im, mi nah trus' 'im, 'im stink.

NIESHA: Why?

ANDREA: Mi jus' met da man las' week an' 'im call mi every day like 'im stalk mi. 'Im always mus' fi know wha' mi do an' where mi be. It too much, man!

NIESHA: Maybe his jus' showin' interes'.

ANDREA: Mi cyan watch 'im. Mi need fi start lookin' far a new place.

NIESHA: Fings getting' bad wif de lan'lord?

ANDREA: She raise up da rent from five 'undred tuh seven 'undred dolla exac'ly when h'Yvonne cut back fi mi hours. She gimmie til mont end fi fine 'er money ar fine a new place.

NIESHA: Bu' da'iz nex wik (next week).

ANDREA: Ur tellin' me?

NIESHA: What you goin' an do?

ANDREA: Mi nah know. Mi prob'ly coulda mek it up dis 'ere mont an' a' look 'bout new place far nex mont, buh da ooman come in ta mi room las' night… in ta mi room! An' search frew all a mi tings an' threat me. 'Bout 'ow come mi can affard fi buy mi nice, sexy tings buh mi cyan' affard fi pay 'er more rent? Maybe mi should look 'bout sellin' some a' mi outfit tuh mek up da money. So, mi cuss 'er! Mi cuss 'er aff. Mi cuss har suh 'ard mi nah even 'memba wha' an wha mi sey—she stan' dere 'old (hold) on tuh 'er crucifix chain— damn 'ypocrite! Bitch, wha' would Jesus do? 'Ow dare she come a' fi mi bedroom an' guh frew fi mi tings! An' 'er comment was suh dotish! Even if mi sell all mi shiny legging an' sequence bra, dem still nah mek up da money fi pay wha' mi owe 'er. Mi tell har tuh get 'er wrinkle ass out a' mi bedroom an' if she come back, she get it way worse dan mi jus' give it tuh 'er.

NIESHA: Ani!

ANDREA: Wha?! "Slut!" She call mi back. She say, she neva di like da idea a' keep a 'arlot (harlot) inna 'er house anyway. Ooo even fuckin say dat word?

NIESHA: You let her tell you dem fings dere?

ANDREA: Mi!? Mi tell 'er, ooo da fuck she tink she be? Maybe a trip out shapping wit me would a gud fi 'er. Maybe if she fresh up 'er style fi 'er husban' woulda keep him eyes where dem suppose tuh be a' stop wanderin' down tuh me.

NIESHA: He mek a moves on you?

ANDREA: Of course! Look 'pan me. Everyone wan' fi mek a move pan mi! Buh, mi nah tell har. Mi let hart ink sey wha' she wan'... No chance she mek me fi stay dere now.

NIESHA: Doesn' look like.

ANDREA: Suh mi move on! Dere not da only place fi rent a' Canada.

NIESAH Bess you don' start fyah (fire) wif no more persons. Is too dangerous.

ANDREA: Everyting a' dangerous! Tell mi wha' not dangerous about da entire situation?

NIESHA: Mek sure you keep your passport and I.D. on you at all times.

ANDREA: A' mi bag. Always a' mi bag!

NIESHA: Good. Don' leave noffing crucial like dat lyin' around dat house.

ANDREA: Passpart one ting mi always fi keep secure.

NIESHA: Good. Da' iz good. Bes you try get out from dere soon as possible.

ANDREA: Already start look.

NIESHA: If you nid to stay wif me part-time, you'a welcome to do so.

ANDREA: Stay were? In di miggle (middle) a da livin' room? Brown couch.

NIESHA: No, brown couch is my own. You can mek yourself on Persian rug.

ANDREA: E' fi sound fancier anyway; Purrrrrrrsian! Where a Persia? Next place a mi fi go a' Persia.

NIESHA: Luxury at it fine' es.

ANDREA: Neva mind. Ur lan'lord wouldna like yuh fi tek in stray.

NIESHA: You not a stray. But you right; I dere offar'in more dan I have in my power to give.

ANDREA: Let's close up.

NIESHA: Closin'!

ANDREA: Where 'im tek yuh?

NIESHA: Don' know. We just have to discuss some final weddin details.

ANDREA: Gud. Mi 'appy far yuh (happy for you).

NIESHA: You gonna be dere (there)?

ANDREA: Already buy mi dress an' it fyah! You watch; Eldrick guh turn 'round an' marry me!

Enter ELDRICK

ELDRICK: Evening.

ANDREA: Eve'lin, Eldricks.

ELDRICK: What's up Andrea?

ANDREA: Mi jus' a leave out.

ELDRICK: No need to rush. Want me to drop you somewhere?

ANDREA: No need.

ELDRICK: You sure?

ANDREA: Bus.

NIESHA smiles. ANDREA exits. NIESHA locks the door behind her.

ELDRICK: Hey.

NIESHA: Hey. Everyfing set?

ELDRICK: Mostly. Just figuring out invitations.

NIESHA: We invitin' people, nuh? I fought it was a low-key fing.

ELDRICK: Iz more for immigration; to make fings look legit. But ya, we can invite some people; not more dan ten.

NIESHA: Who we should invite?

ELDRICK: Well, we nid two witness; some family and friends would be okay. Only people we trust.

NIESHA: Only Andrea and my aunty, I have.

ELDRICK: Great— How about Yvonne or Donnie or Charlene? Donnie's cool.

NIESHA: No. Nobody from de restaurant.

ELDRICK: Your aunty can be your witness, den? I'll axe one of my padnas to be mine.

NIESHA: Bes' use Ani, oui, for me. I not sure my aunty will come. You inviting any of your family?

ELDRICK: I do not know.

NIESHA: Why not?

ELDRICK: Iz not really de type of wedding I'd want to invite dem to.

NIESHA: What's wrong wif it?

ELDRICK: Niesha, iz jus a quick fing. We can have a real wedding another time and invite all the people we want.

NIESHA: Dat don' always happem, wha' if we only have dis one?

ELDRICK: Well den, dis is de one we have.

Beat.

Dere will be flowers an' stuff. I'm paying a girl to do decorations; it will be fine.

NIESHA: Okay. So, you will sen' invitations out tomorrow, or what?

ELDRICK: Yeah, give me Ani and your aunty address.

NIESHA: Bes' you just give me Ani own in my hand.

Beat.

Maybe I'll invite my roommate too. I don' know, maybe not. Iz too risky.

ELDRICK: Up to you. Just let me know soon so I can print more invitations.

NIESHA: Okay.

ELDRICK: Oh, 'member I said I'd nid some change to cover de weddin' coss' an' immigration expense an' dat?

NIESHA: Yes.

ELDRICK: I got de number work out reasonable but am gonna need it soon.

NIESHA: Okay. How much?

ELDRICK: Ten fousand.

NIESHA: Dollars?

ELDRICK: Yeh.

NIESHA: Ten fousand dollars?!

ELDRICK: Most people I know told me it cossin' fifteen or twenty fousand but I don' need all dat. Just a likkle to cover my upfront coss'. You have to invest somefing, oddawise you could change your mind, run off and am lef wif all de coss', understand?

NIESHA: Coss', qui sa (what's that)?

ELDRICK: Or de cops could come and arrest you today, den am stuck with de debt, you see?

NIESHA: What exac'ly you nid ten fousand dollars for?

ELDRICK: What I need it for? You serious?

NIESHA: When have I ever been joking?

ELDRICK: What happen' to trus'?

NIESHA: If you tell me what you nid all dat money for, you will fine de trus' come back.

ELDRICK: Okay, filing de papers for you and your kids is gonna cost me about free fousand.

NIEHSA Why?

ELDRICK: De fees, Niesha. Have you looked at de fees chart? I can show it to you if you want.

NIESHA: Yes, plis.

ELDRICK: I don' have it on me, obviously. I didn't come here finking I was going to have to explain everyfing in detail to my fianceé who suppose to truss me.

NIESHA: Fine. Carry on.

ELDRICK: I have a guy who's gonna take care of de papers for us, but we have to pay him up front. You don' want to mess with these types of things; always better to leave it in de hands of people who know what dey doing. I know nuff people who he set up nice.

NIESHA: Okay, what else?

ELDRICK: I went really minimal with de wedding; I didn't spend noffing on noffing fancy, but remember, it has to look real otherwise the government won't believe. Even a bare minimum wedding, like what I did, costs free fousand dollars and add. Can you see how it all add up?

NIESHA: De res' of it?

ELDRICK: I tol' you to truss me. Now you're coming wid all dese questions?

NIESHA: You tol' me you didn't want noffing from me.

ELDRICK: I'm not taking noffing from you; all dis is for you!

NIESHA: I have a right to know what kine of man am getting involve wif.

ELDRICK: Okay. I am responsible for you and your two kids for free years. Free (three) people, for free years! I need to have some money in case any of you get sick and nid medical treatments—even small fings like dental bills; I don't have insurance to cover dat. Anyfing you give me now, will come back to benefit you in de end.

NIESHA: An' some of it goin' an line your pocket as well.

ELDRICK: What?

NIESHA: Not to shit me, Eldricks!

ELDRICK: Are you serious?

NIESHA: Dis arrangement clearly benefiting you more dan it do me.

ELDRICK: How?

NIESHA: You did tell me you want to do me a favour—

ELDRICK: I do.

NIESHA: And dere was noffing you did want—

ELDRICK: I told you dere would be a small fee—

NIESHA: Small? Dere is no way all of what you mention dere coming up to $10,000.

Some of it is you directly benefiting from me. Admit dat.

ELDRICK: No.

NIESHA: Yes! Yes, it is.

ELDRICK: I told you, when I came dere, someone did me a favour. You fink dat was for free? Noffing came easy for me. Ten years I been here workin' odd labour jobs; goin' where de money is. Sometimes I does go wiks and am dry— no work, but I survivin', still, noffing is easy.

I know countless people who have done dis, some of dem are still married to dis day and dey happy. Nobody I know or heard of ever did do it for free. Iz just not de way it works; I fought you knew.

NIESHA: I had faif dat good people exist who don' want noffing but to see good for odders.

ELDRICK: You fink I don' want to see good for you?

NIESHA: I heard of people who did do dis for free for no odda reason but dey loving, good heart.

ELDRICK: Where you heard dat? Back home in Fanon? You prob'ly also heard money does grows on trees and der strits are lined wif gold.

NIESHA: You did tell me you love me—

ELDRICK: I do love you—

NIESHA: —an' dat all you wanted was to have me as a wife. Which now, looking back, I cannot believe I be—

ELDRICK —Come on, all of dat is true. Why you acting— After all I done for you? I cannot believe— I love you, yes, I do, but I also have to protect myself. Why can't you understan dat? One does not cancel out de odder.

Beat.

NIESHA: Where I gettin dat kine of money, Eldricks?

ELDRICK: Don't you have savings?

NIESHA: I have chir'ren. You know how much I makin'.

ELDRICK: You can borrow it and pay it back later.

NIESHA: Who you fink have dat kine of money flexible to give me?

ELDRICK: Dere are people who can help you out, you just gotta know who to talk to.

NIESHA: I suppose you know who dose people are?

ELDRICK: I can find out. But also, you have your aunt, and dere's a Cash Money right dere. A Money Mart on de odder side if you don' like it.

NIEHSA You know I canna go to dem places dere.

ELDRICK: Well—

NIESHA: You know dat! Lowa de fee a likkle bit, nuh, Eldricks. Make it five or even six fousand. Please, then I will know you love me.

ELDRICK: I already did lower it. Any odda man out dere would charge you twenty fousand dollars, easy. Now if you want to, you can take your chances and go and look for one of dem. Am not holding you down.

In a few years, when you see de type of life you've been able to give your chir'ren, dis money will be not even be relevant. We'll be happy. And you'll laugh at de fack dat you made such a big commotion over noffing. Fink about people you know who would die for an opportunity like this. I never fink about de money I paid. Iz a sacrifice am glad I did make!

NIESHA: Iz not dat I sayin'—I not goin' an find someone else. Am jus'— you— I nid some time to figure all dis out.

ELDRICK: I was goin' to deliver de invitations today.

NIESHA: I said I nid time.

ELDRICK: Our wedding is nex week—

NIESHA: So, I nid a few days. If I am to pay you, all of it, right now, I need to figure out how am gettin' de money right? If I cannot have a payment plan wif you, I mus' make one wif somebody, right?

ELDRICK: Alright den, I will not pressure you. Take your few days. I did not expeck dis reaction from you. I fought it was a good setup, but I guess I was wrong?

Beat.

NIESHA: Close de door on your way out de shop.

ELDRICK: So, we not going out?

NIESHA: You fink I want to go anywhere wif you, Eldrick; come on!

ELDRICK: At least let me drive you home.

NIESHA: I don' want to see your face right now!

ELDRICK: So how you gonna get home?

NIESHA: Same way I get in work today an' every day.

ELDRICK: Baby, don't ruin dis. I really love you and I don' want to see you go back to Fanon, for what? A few dollars?

NIESHA: Eldrick, not to bodda me right now.

ELDRICK: I'm just trying to remind you—

NIESHA: Bus! I nid to catch de bus.

ELDRICK: Of what you'll be missing if you don't go frew wif dis. Fine, take your few days to let me know what you decide when you ready. It's all about you anyways so…

NIESHA: Close de door on your way out.

ELDRICK: I do love you, Niesha. It doesn't have to be one or de odder.

ELDRICK exits. NIESHA picks up the broom.

Shift. Enter MALCOLM.

MALCOLM: Ani? Niesha, is Ani here?

NIESHA: She did leave a while ago, oui. What you looking for her for? She' not seeing you again.

MALCOLM: I found her bracelet in the back of my car.

NIESHA: It's been nearly two wiks.

MALCOLM: I was just cleaning out the car—and I missed her…you know? I knew I did, but seeing dis thing of hers made me realize— She said she needed some help, I didn't know what kind of help— I didn't listen— I didn't help her. I didn't even axe what she needs; I was having such a good time and she was too, so I couldn't figure what else she would need.

NIESHA: You fought sex in de back of a truck was all a woman nid?

MALCOLM: When it started out, I didn't expec—

NIESHA: Anyway, never mind, none of my business, don' want to know. No sense talking to me—I don' know where she at.

MALCOLM: Is she in trouble?

NIESHA: Of course she in trouble! Everybody in trouble.

MALCOLM: I mean immediate trouble. Like—danger. With the law? Or with another person? I know she tends to run her mouth.

NIESHA: **

MALCOLM: I told her once dat I love her but she didn't believe me. I actually didn't believe me either. But now I can't stop thinking. She looked kinda desperate, you know? Afraid. alone. I don't want that for her. Do you think if I pass by her place?

NIESHA: You bes' not go by where she stay. An' I did tell you I don' know where she is.

Don' axe me to solve your problems.

MALCOLM: I'm not—

NIESHA: Yes! you are! An' I have my own which am figuring out myself an' not axein' any help from you.

MALCOLM: Where do I go if I can't—

NIESHA: I need you to leave. It after nine. Nobody supposed to be in de shop; we closed. I have food I can give you if you want. It's been sitting out all day but it's been in the warmer so...

MALCOLM: Ya. I'll take some food.

NIESHA: Good.

NIESHA goes behind the counter and fills a white container with food.

Here's all I got. Take it. Here.

She hands him the container of food.

MALCOLM: Give me two pop.

NIESHA: What flavour?

MALCOLM: Purple Crush and… ginger ale.

NIESHA hands the two cans to him.

How much?

NIESHA: Jus' give me two dollars for de pops.

He hands her the two dollars and pushes the ginger ale toward her.

MALCOLM: Extra one was for you.

I'm sorry I missed her, Niesha. I would offer you a ride home, but you've never taken me up and I suspect you won't start now.

NISHA I don' finish close up; I would not want to keep you waiting.

MALCOLM: I don't mind—

NIESHA: I don'—

MALCOLM lingers for a few moments, then exits. NIESHA takes a beat to compose herself then turns the chairs over the table.

ACT II

An empty Niagara Falls hotel room. It should stay empty for some time. Sound of two sets of formal shoes coming down the hallway and NIESHA on the phone.

NIESHA: *(From off.)* You're breakin' up... ya, de wifi here not de best. Where her? Well, who an' who goin and find out?

Enter NIESHA in a wedding dress; ELDRICK in a suit kissing her neck and trying to undress her.

Okay, okay, okay— Pat, I can ring you back? Lata? Okay den.

She hangs up.

ELDRICK: You finally done wif de phone?

NIESHA: I guess so.

ELDRICK: Good.

He tosses it.

Put it out of our sight for a few hours. Whole night, you more interested in your phone dan your husban'.

NIESHA: I nided to get in touch wif someone from Andrea family.

ELDRICK: Right now, dough? Dat's what I don' get.

NIESHA: I was worried. I don' know where she be.

ELDRICK: I already told you, she in de jailhouse with all de rest of de deportees—

NIESHA: No!

ELDRICK: Yeh. And she'll still be dere tomorrow and der next day, so—

NIESHA: Dey really does put dem in jail?

ELDRICK: Where else do you think dey does be? Luxury hotel?

NIESHA: Try I tryin' not to fink about Ani in jail!

ELDRICK: Den don' fink about it. Fink of who is in front of you.

NIESHA: *******

Beat.

I hungry.

ELDRICK: You just ate.

NIESHA: I feel like I goin an pass out. You fink I relly enjoy dat food you call "cat-er-in?" Where you fin' dem food dere, anywayz? De broccoli was sof sof sof, like de puree dey does give ol' people wif no teef in dey mouf. And de chicken wasn' tase'in nice— not even a pinch of salt.

ELDRICK: You know what, am hungry, too.

NIESHA: Where we can get some West Indian food?

ELDRICK: I know a place. Don't know if iz still open—

NIESHA: Go check, nuh?

ELDRICK: Okay. Don't miss me too much.

He kisses her.

Shift. Two days ago. ANDREA appears at Jerk Pork Castle. Though still in the hotel room, NIESHA talks to her as if she's there in real time.

NIESHA: How de house huntin' goin'?

ANDREA: Girl, ee nah gud. It h'expensive! Mi nah know 'ow prices gone up so 'igh in jus' a few shart mont! Mi start lookin' from las' week an' cyan't find nuh decent room fi under six 'undred!

NIESHA: Dat's not bad.

ANDREA: Right now, mi pay five 'undred!

NIESHA: Buh you know you cy'an stay where you be right now.

ANDREA: Might 'ave fi tek you up an' stay pan Persian rug.

NIESHA: Two hundred doe'la.

ANDREA: Yuh wan fi charge me fi sleep on yur stinkin' floor?

NIESHA: Eh eh! Fings hard!

ANDREA laughs. Disappearing.

Shift. Hotel room. Present.

Enter ELDRICK with two paper bags in his hands.

ELDRICK: Stupid paper bags— Shit, man! De grease drip up all on my suit!

NIESHA: You reach dere quick.

ELDRICK: Dey didn't have jerk chicken, so I got two fing of jerk pork.

NIESHA: I don' like jerk pork, nah.

ELDRICK: You work at Jerk Pork Castle.

NIESHA: An' dat's why I don' eatin' dat!

ELDRICK: Eat up de rice den. I make dem put extra chicken gravy—

NIESHA: De chicken finish buh dey still had chicken gravy?

ELDRICK: Yeh. It happens some time.

NIESHA: So wuh you give me dere is jerk pork wif chicken gravy?

ELDRICK: Yeh. Dat's what I said.

NIESHA: Leave it dere.

ELDRICK: You're not goin' an' eat it?

NIESHA: I will take it when am ready.

ELDRICK: I pass by a liquor store on my way. Dere's a small fing of rum an' a bokkle of Cokes. Mix yourself a drink.

NIESHA: I don' drink.

ELDRICK: It will help you to loosen up.

NIESHA: I don' drink!

ELDRICK: Listen, Niesha, I don' know wha' dat wrong wif you— Your walk down de aisle looked like a deaf (death) walk. You did not dance wif me at all during de reception. When you said "I do" you looked like you might pull a knife and cut me up. All in der elevator, I been trying to get close to you; loosen you up. Since we got in de door—

I expected dat when I came back from der store— at least—we could have a fresh try at dis husband and wife fing. It would had been nice to find you, maybe lyin' down across der bed like dey do in de movies. You coulda put dat nice likkle lingerie fing I did buy you.

NIESHA: You bought?!

ELDRICK: I paid good money for dis hotel room—

NIESHA: You paid?

ELDRICK: For us to enjoy on our honeymoon—

NIESHA: Ho-ney-moon?

ELDRICK: Wedding night—

NIESHA: Wed-ding night? Honeymoon? You paid?!

ELDRICK: Yes! And I expected dat you would be a likkle more… nice dan you have been de entire day.

NIESHA: An' you fought drinks would help me do dat? I don' wan' to drink. Drinkin' makes people ugly inside an' out. It makin' you behave bad an' act like a damn fool. Make your hair fall off, skin grey, rottin' all your teef an' give you a big ol'. gut for you to be rel unattractive. It nasty an' I won't do it!

ELDRICK pours himself half a cup full of rum and significantly less Coke, mixes it with a stir stick and takes a drink.

ELDRICK: If you hungry, why you don't eat den?

NIESHA: Jus' now.

ELDRICK: What if I feed you?

He opens up one of the containers of food, a plastic fork and knife and goes over to sit with NIESHA. He scrapes the jerk pork to the side and feeds her the rice. She lets him feed her.

NIESHA: Stop pushin' food in my mouf; I don' like it an' I don' want it!

She feeds herself.

You scraped de jerk pork buh it still mix in de whole stupid food.

Beat.

How long dey keep dem in de jail? De deportees.

ELDRICK: I don't know, six to eight monfs, free to five years. Sometimes less if you can get someone to bail you out.

NIESHA: How much is it for bail?

ELDRICK: Depends. Usually between ten to twenty fousand. Not many people have dat lying around.

NIESHA: You do.

ELDRICK: Niesha.

NIESHA: You do!

ELDRICK: Look, I already tol' you what I nided dat money for, so you nid to finish wif it.

NIESHA: You did not use all out of it.

ELDRICK: I used more of it dan I should have on a wedding day dat I didn't enjoy and a wedding night dat it doesn't look like is going to go much better.

NIESHA: Wha' dere to enjoy? You relly expec' me to believe dat wedding cost free fousand dollas? On what you spend de money, nuh? De flowers? What flowers? My bouquet look like somefing Ani buy from hukter in de Pickerin' flea.

ELDRICK: Your dress, de décor, de food?

NIESHA: Dé-cor!?

ELDRICK: Yes!

NIESHA: Dose shits (sheets) you had hangin' downg from de ceiling? Dem Christmas light?

ELDRICK: Dose shits cost me five hundred, plus someone had to hang dem and dem lights.

NIESHA: What I was supposed to enjoy? My one guest? My aunty who fink she betta dan me? My ordder guest—my only frien'—lock in deportee jail for two days an' I have not heard from her? An' de food—where you order dat food? All day long, I dere tryin' to sort out on which items you pour out my money.

ELDRICK: Am not going to explain to you again—

NIESHA: You don' expec' me to believe you spend it on de camera man, who was clearly one of your boozer friends who you just chose because he have a alright camera phone. What he goin' an do to edit my pictures? Put filter? Cat eyes? Bunny nose?

ELDRICK: Dose boozer pictures are going to prove you had a real legitimate wedding.

NIESHA: I know! Dat's why you could have hired a better—I nid dose pictures to look good, Eldrick!

ELDRICK: I know.

NIESHA: I don' have no ordder option; I nid for dis to work.

ELDRICK: Yes ma'am; I get de message.

Shift. Two days ago. JPC. Same as before.

ANDREA: Since Persian rug e' now out a' my league, mi 'affi figure out someting.

NIESHA: A lady living across my aunty want to rent out her one-bedroom basement.

ANDREA: One bedroom as in private?

NIESHA: Private.

ANDREA: Wit a bat'room?

NIESHA: An' a tub.

ANDREA: Oooh! Dat nice.

NIESHA: Yeh, but eight hundred dolla she want.

ANDREA: Ooo.

NIESHA: But iz private. Private entrance, bafroom, kitchen an' de door lockin'.

ANDREA: Door lack...

No one nah go inna my tings…

Ya, but eight 'undred.

NIESHA: If iz de best you can get, I could leave where I am an' come live wif you.

ANDREA: Den it wouldna be private.

NIESHA: Private enough.

ANDREA: Yuh nah fi live wid me, Niesha.

NIESHA: Why not?

ANDREA: Becaw every time yuh put da news pon da TV, mi wan' fi' pile up chairs, climb up, wrinch dat a' TV an' smash it down a' da floor. If mi' 'ad fi listen tuh dat inna mi 'ome also, listen tuh you a' tell mi mi a' talk too loud or mi up too late or yuh cyan' stand mi music, mi a' suffocate. If me a' you fi tek a one bedroom, ooo would get da bedroom? Huh? You becaw yuh fine da place an' mi fi get stuck on da floor—yuh always come out an top some'ow and mi can't figure out 'ow yuh do it.

NIESHA: We could share de room—we could share de bed if we have to.

ANDREA: Nuh tank yuh. Yuh 'ave a good setup, nah mess it up fi me. Soon you a guh live wit ur 'usband, so…

NIESHA: Dat's true; I min, I could axe Eldricks—

ANDREA: Nuh, tanks! Mi nah share bedroom wit a newlywed couple—nuh uh!

NIESHA: Iz not goin' an be like dat.

ANDREA: Why it nah be like dat?

NIESHA: I going at de back to change. You good at de front?

ANDREA: Yeh, mi a chap up da salads.

Shift. Present.

ELDRICK is unlacing NIESHA's wedding dress. He kisses her back. Tenderness. NIESHA seems like she's into it for a while, then pushes him off.

NIESHA: Woahta (water)! Woahta! I chokin'!

ELDRICK: Really? First you're hungry, now you're firsty.

NIESHA: I'll go for it myself.

She gets up and gets a cup of water from the bathroom.

ELDRICK: I don't know what's wrong wif you.

NIESHA: I need to bave (bathe).

ELDRICK heads to the bathroom.

ELDRICK: Yo, I didn' even watch de bafroom! Nice big tub in dere.

NIESHA: For one.

ELDRICK: Really?

NIESHA: I want to bave by myself.

ELDRICK: Oh, come on—

NIESHA: Why you don' take a walk outside an' see de falls.

ELDRICK: It's kinda a lovers ting.

NIESHA: Yeh, so you should go—

ELDRICK: We'll go later. Togeda (together).

Put dis on when you come out de baf.

He throws lingerie at her. NIESHA enters the bathroom closes the door and turns on the tap.

Shift. JPC. Last week.

NIESHA: Not to worry Ani; you will fine' a place. You know, Canada can fit Fanon one hundred time inside it? And maybe Caviva free hundred! I went an drive de ordder day wif Eldricks; dreamin' of a place of our own to live, an' we drive out to a place, where we were driving an' driving an' couldn't see no house! Dere have places in dis country wif waterfalls an' mountain bigger dan in eidder of our countries! Dere are wide fields an' acres an' acres of untouched land. Dis country so big, huge! Cannot tell me dere isn't room for you and me to stay in it an' find our place.

Shift. Present.

ELDRICK on the bed watching TV. NIESHA comes out of the bathroom, still fully dressed.

ELDRICK: You not gonna bave again?

NIESHA: Change my mind.

ELDRICK: You want company, or…?

NIESHA: **

ELDRICK: Okay, Niesha, cut it, okay? You want to finish wif dis? You want to leave and I cut up your papers and we finish wif dis? I not spen'in two years here miserable wif you, okay? You are a grown woman! You gonna let money get in de way of somefing we have dat is goin' on good? You paid me de money, so what, I nided it, I promise to set you up in return, what are you gonna do about it now? We are in love, I can make you happy; we agreed about dat. We can have more kids if you want—you want dat and it's possible, but I nid you to relax.

NIESHA: On one hand, I can count de amount of people I trust in my whole life! My modder, Yvonne, my first child fadder, my sister, and Ani. But for some reason, you gave me a feeling like I could trus' you.

You came to me as if— I wanted somefing and you were my oppa'tunity, my blessing from God, so I didn't question it. You told me dere would be money, fine, I was prepared to pay a likkle bit.

When you came to de store axein' me for all what I had save, plus more—I relly consider it because—look at de oppa'tunity! I fought, if I get a loan from somebody here, borrow from my aunty dere, take out all what in my savings, I could make it—it could be a good deal. But den I fought, no, dis man say he love me an' when people are in love dey don' steal or take advantage of bad situation. Just two days ago, I was ready to take de phone an' tell you exactly where you could take your offer, an' go! I was finking, maybe I could take my chances an' stay. See if I could find anodder way in. I could get legitimate work, talk to more people, I don' know, try my luck—I had better plans for my money dan givin' it all to you.

But den, I was at de back changin' my cloddes (clothes) an' Andrea was at de front cuttin' salad when de police come.

JPC. Two days ago. NIESHA stays in present.

OFFICER: Morning, I'm looking for Miss Andrea Blackmore.

ANDREA: Dis is she.

NIESHA: She didn't even lie.

OFFICER: Ma'am, I'm going to have to ask you to come with us.

ANDREA: Alright.

NIESHA: She didn't put up no fight.

OFFICER: You are under arrest for violating the terms of your Temporary Resident Visitor Visa.

ANDREA: **

Present.

NIESHA: And den de door open, an' de door close. An' she had gone wif dem. And I, as a coward, stayed in de back behind de fridge poking my eyes to see frew de glass. When I see her, handcuff an' duckin into police ve'cle, last fing I saw was—she didn't look frighten. I would had been frighten—but she look like she wa' ready for whatever was about to happen while I crouch behind de fridge.

And den my mine res' on you an' how just moments before I was finking—I hated you! But when I saw Andrea and I saw how quickly everyfing dat we had work for, all our hope could be stuff down de back of a police ve'cle, I grab my phone quick quick quick an' tol' you— Yes, I've had some time to fink an'— Yes! Send de invitations, I get de money—it's not too late? Am ready; sorry for de delay…

ELDRICK: You made de right choice.

NIESHA: Yeh.

ELDRICK: Not everyone gets lucky like you and me—we bit (beat) de system!

NIESHA: I know.

ELDRICK: You know, how many people out dere hiding to keep undda de radar? You could be here twenty years and once dey find you, boom, you're gone. You don' have to worry about dat again.

NIESHA: I realize.

ELDRICK: I am in dis wif you for life, koprann (understand)?

NIESHA: Yep.

ELDRICK: So we need to be happy, understand?

NIESHA moves to the dressing table, takes off her earrings and puts them down. She takes off her shoes.

She takes off her stockings; she struggles to undo her dress. He comes to her to help her with the buttons.

See? I want to be a good man to you.

She allows him to finish unbuttoning her dress; it falls.

A suspended moment.

NIESHA: I nid to call my kids.

ELDRICK: Call your kids when you are done.

NIESHA: No.

ELDRICK: You don' know what you want.

NIESHA: ***

ELDRICK: You don' want me?

NIESHA: I…

ELDRICK: I can give you and your children a nice comfortable life and you never have to see the back of Fanon again, so…

NIESHA: **

ELDRICK: So, what?

NIESHA: What, Eldricks? What?

ELDRICK: I would not hurt you, Niesha.

Long beat.

NIESHA: I relly need to call my chirren.

ELDRICK: Again, wif your urgent fings dat cannot wait?

NIESHA: I could love you if you could be a good fadder—

ELDRICK: Niesha, go on; de choice is yours—

She dials.

NIESHA: Hi Abby? It's Mom. It's all done now; I married today. He's okay *(Referencing ELDRICK.)* — I miss you all too. Tell your brodder jus' wait; am trying my best. Okay. Love you all, too.

End.